Glass Half Full

Ian White

978-0-646-83050-6
© 2020. Ian J. White
All rights reserved

First published December 2020
Second Edition February 2021
Third Edition April 2023

No part of this book may be reproduced or transmitted in any form or by any means, graphic, electronic, or mechanical, including photocopying, without the written permission from the publisher.

Published by the author, in association with IngramSpark, Melbourne

I remember my affliction and my wandering,
the bitterness, and the gall.
I well remember them, and my soul is downcast within me.
Yet this I call to mind and therefore I have hope:
Because of the LORD's great love, we are not consumed,
for his compassions never fail.
They are new every morning;
great is your faithfulness. I say to myself,
"The LORD is my portion;
therefore I will wait on Him."

Lamentations 3:19-24 (emphasis added by the author)

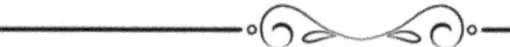

DEDICATION

For my father, James, my best friend,
taken from us far too early at the age of 56.
Still love you, Dad. Still miss you every day.

CONTENTS

Acknowledgements   vi

Author's Note   viii

Chapter 1
Planting the Rose Garden   1

Chapter 2
God's Grace is Enough   13

Chapter 3
This Too Shall Pass   33

Chapter 4
Don't Beat Up on Yourself   46

Chapter 5
Be Kind to Yourself   56

Chapter 6
The Sum Total of Many Small Victories   66

Chapter 7
Encouragement   74

Chapter 8
Choose How to Live   92

Chapter 9
When the World Changes   109

Chapter 10
Leave the World a Better Place   124

Chapter 11
Live a Life of Hope   135

Bibliography   147

ACKNOWLEDGEMENTS

Many people, both family and friends, have been of great encouragement to me, not only during the writing of this book but stretching back over many years. There are so many of them that it is foolhardy to try and list them here. But I do want to list some of them; people who love me, and pray for me, and who have supported and encouraged me in many ways. They include my cousins Diane Clulow and Lynette Prince, my wonderful friends Rod and Sue Davidson, Don and Heather McGregor, Rev. Frank Willis and Barbara Willis, and Rev. Dr Michael O'Neil and Rev. Monica O'Neil. There are many others and although not mentioned here they know that their names are inscribed on my heart. You know who you are, and I am so grateful for your love and encouragement over the years. And now, this is pay-back time for me; an opportunity for me to encourage others, through my writing.

I particularly want to thank my dear friend Ruth Warwick. I first met Ruth and her family when I was living in Western Australia. We worshiped at the same church and over the years a warm friendship developed between the Warwick family and me. Ruth is dedicated to counselling people who suffer from a mental illness and to helping them regain the joy that has been stolen from their lives. Ruth also runs regular workshops and seminars to help educate carers, those who need to care for family and loved ones who suffer from a mental illness. Ruth's work in the mental health field is critically important within the community and is characterised by her grace and by her love for others. I admire her work in a field about which I know truly little and so, when I found myself needing to write about mental health in this book, my thoughts turned immediately to Ruth. Those sections of the book which deal with the management of mental health issues were proofread by Ruth, and I cannot find adequate words to express my gratitude to her for her comments, corrections, and suggestions which have helped to make this a better book. Thank you, Ruth.

I again thank my good friend Danny Tedeshi of *Inlingua Text* for the preparation of the artwork files for the covers on this book. When I need artwork, of any kind, I always turn to Danny for that work because I know of his exceptional talents in graphic design and typesetting. Thank you for your great work, Danny.

The Holy Spirit is the driving and guiding force in all that I do and write. Without the impetus of the Holy Spirit, I would not have even thought about writing this book. During the process of writing and fine-tuning this book I constantly prayed that my thoughts and words would be guided by the Spirit. It is my hope, and my prayer, that the joy of Jesus Christ and the encouragement of the Holy Spirit will shine through my writing for the blessing of all who read it.

Ian J. White
December 2020

AUTHORS' NOTE

Don't think that you have picked up a book written by a guy who believes that he's got it all together, and who can't wait to tell you how you can get it all together. You have not! I have found much of my life to be a real rollercoaster ride, times of great joy and times of great sadness, times of elation and times of hopelessness, times of great confidence and times of doubt and introspection. I have lived through times of absolute peace and certainty, and through times of emotional turmoil. I have known times of optimism and certainty, and times spent wondering where on earth we are going, and asking myself "What's the point of it all?"

And, as I am sure you well know, I am not unique. Most people in the world, dare I say *all* people, live life on the rollercoaster; peaks and troughs, euphoria – despondency – euphoria. This is a beautiful world, but it is not a perfect world; it is a world in which we will, and do, find ourselves hurting in the low part of the ride; the troughs. And although some of those troughs are self-induced, in the main they are not; they are just the low point through which the rollercoaster carries us on its way to the next peak.

What I want to do with this book is to encourage every reader to be ever looking upward, with hope, towards that next peak. Although my writing comes from the perspective of a follower of Jesus Christ, and draws upon the Holy Scriptures in places, it sets out to be an encouragement for all readers, for Christian and for non-Christian readers alike. Fundamentally, we are all on that rollercoaster but, also, we are all here to live life in abundance and joy, as promised by Jesus.

There is little point in trying to fight the rollercoaster, it goes where the tracks lead, but if we can live in harmony with the rollercoaster's rhythm, then we can live life with joy and with optimism, knowing that the rollercoaster will carry us to another peak. There will still be troughs, we will have troubles, that's part of living in an imperfect world, a fallen world, but when we look at the beauty of life as seen from the peaks, the troughs become bearable.

As I have said, I write from the Christian perspective. I hope that you, the reader, also have the confidence that we get from knowing Jesus Christ. But whether you are a Christian or not, I hope and pray that you will find joy, hope, and optimism in these pages.

Optimism is real. It is real and it is of crucial importance, for without optimism we might drown in those troughs. It is my hope and my prayer that every reader will find the encouragement of this book to be real in their lives and that they will know the joy that comes through living this God-given life.

Life is beautiful. The glass is half full. May you find it so.

Ian J. White
December 2020.

Chapter 1
Planting the Rose Garden

With few exceptions, the true Christian, living in the power and the joy of the Holy Spirit, is an eternal optimist. He lives his life as if he knows that his future is assured, which it is, and as if he is living a God-given life, which he is, in a world which although far from perfect still reflects the glory and the beauty of God's good creation. Whilst living in the present and recognising that this present world is not perfect, he/she lives with the sure and certain knowledge that God has promised to renew everything, including our very selves; to make everything new again so that it will be as perfect as it was in the beginning. And, in the meantime, the Christian optimist is encouraged by catching glimpses of how it will be in God's perfect New Creation. There are also, of course, non-Christian optimists; people with a cheery disposition and a belief that everything will turn out all right in the end. One must wonder, however, whether non-Christian optimism is based on anything other than wishful thinking and blind trust in an unknown future, an exercise in mental fantasy. Even so, such a position is better than pessimism. If you, the reader, are a non-Christian and an optimist, I do not mean to denigrate you and your optimism, but perhaps it might be an opportune time for you to consider what your optimism is based upon.

Are there Christian pessimists? There should not be but, sadly, there are. People who have come into a saving relationship with God through grace and through faith in Jesus Christ, and yet people who have allowed the joy to have been permanently stolen from their lives. Somehow, through ways that I do not fully understand, the evil one, the great joy-stealer, has managed to infiltrate their lives and to impact their worldview. I will give you a very personal example of this shortly.

At the same time, we must acknowledge that Christian optimists do, at times, go through very difficult situations which might take away their joy for a time, and when that happens, they may be severely tested and may struggle with their faith for any of a number of reasons, and in later chapters we are going to look at how Christians can find themselves in these situations. At such times Christians may descend into a pessimistic state of mind, for a season, but that is not their natural home. It must be said, also, that Christians and non-Christians alike can, and often do, suffer from clinical depression and anxiety, a very real and debilitating form of mental illness. Again, much will be said about this in a later chapter. Notwithstanding those difficult seasons which we may experience in our lives, and the possible actuality of mental illness, for most Christians our fall-back position, our default position if you like, is one of optimism rooted firmly in the promises of God.

True pessimists, however, live their lives with a different default position, one which cannot see the joy of a God-given life and the beauty of this world. They cannot see a positive future for their lives or for the world at large, or at least if they do see it, they choose not to acknowledge it. From my observations there appear to be two kinds of pessimists; what I categorise as 'thinking pessimists' and 'non-thinking pessimists'.

The non-thinking pessimists are the ones who just do not see the positives of life, they do not look for the positives, in fact they seem almost incapable of such thoughts. And sadly, amongst their number there are some Christians. I find that sad, and partly because I have experienced this in a very personal way. You see, my own mother was such a person. My mother, who I must say that I loved dearly, lived to the age of 97. Mother had to be in the full-time care of a nursing home for the last six months of her life, but until that time she lived independently. My father died at an early age, some 40 years earlier than mother, and so she spent a lot of time living alone, apart from those times when she visited myself or my sister, or when we were visiting her. Thus, it is reasonable to say that hers was not an easy or, in some ways a fulfilling life, and that may have contributed to her sense of pessimism. Whether it was the death of my father at an early age that triggered her pessimism I cannot say, but from that time onwards I cannot remember seeing her smile other than when being asked to smile for the camera and even then, it was more of a grimace than a smile.

Yes, she was frail for many years, yes, she lived with a lot of constant pain for many years, and yes, I get that, but when I say that I cannot remember the last time that I saw her smile I am talking of a period of more than 40 years. It was a source of immense and constant frustration to me that she just could not respond to things positively and could not see the love and the beauty that surrounded her. She had only negative thoughts. It seemed that she was always looking for, and expecting, bad things to eventuate. Indeed, I sometimes wondered whether she *desired* bad things to happen. There were times when I thought that I must be the stupidest person in the world because I cannot recall suggesting something to which she did not respond with up to a dozen reasons why it would not work. Don't get me wrong; as I have said I did love her very much and, now that she has passed, I miss her greatly. She was a Christian, she loved the Lord, but it was well hidden beneath a veil of outward pessimism.

Perhaps you, too, know some non-thinking pessimists, people who never think about the joy and the wonder of a God-given life. The reason is simple; they are incapable of such thoughts. I tried for many years to talk to my mother about the joy and happiness which Jesus wants us to have and to live, and it saddened me greatly that I did so without any success. If you are trying to help a person with a similar disposition, I empathise with you. I know the difficulty you face, and I can only hope and pray that you have more success than I did.

The thinking pessimist, on the other hand, is at least capable of seeing wonderful and beautiful things in this world. Whilst he or she generally holds fast to a pessimistic view of circumstances around them, and a pessimistic worldview of the future, he/she does at least recognise that others approach life differently. And that causes a dilemma for the thinking pessimist because such people look at the optimist and worry that the optimist just may be right. Worries? Yes, deep down they worry, because they fear that they might be missing out on something which is not only important, but valuable beyond all else. And, in this, they are right. The good news, though, is that the thinking pessimist can change and can become an optimist. We know that can happen for various reasons, but it especially happens, of course, when one meets Jesus Christ.

Now, at this point I am going to assume that you, the reader, are an optimist, that whether you are a Christian or not, like me you are a glass-half-full person. I reach that conclusion based on the not unreasonable assumption that if you were a pessimist you would likely have stopped reading before getting to this point. So, let us move forward now, positively, with optimism and with passion.

The true optimist, Christian or non-Christian, does not simply drift through life with the mindset that the world is becoming a better and more just place. Rather, they actively live life not only knowing that is the case, but also knowing that they are part of that process and that they can, and should, work actively and passionately to ensure that they help to make it so. That doesn't mean that to be an optimist you need to give up your day job, but it does mean putting your optimism on public display and employing your passions in life for the betterment of the world at large; at the office, within your family life, within your social club, within your church, within your circle of friends, within the community of your local neighbourhood, indeed anywhere and everywhere that you might venture. And when we live that way an amazing thing happens; optimism is contagious! Not always, it must be said, for you may encounter a non-thinking pessimist such as my own mother but, by and large, people respond to one's optimism with a more positive and forward-looking mindset than they might otherwise have had. I am a firm believer in the credo that optimism begets optimism, and that passion begets passion! We emulate optimists and people of passion, not because they are an example and an inspiration to us, though they are, but because they give rise within us of our own innate desire and passion to create goodness.

Most people have things in life about which they are passionate. At least, I should say, that I think that all optimists, Christian and non-Christian optimists alike, have things about which they are passionate. Can that be said of pessimists? I do not know, and the reason that I don't know is that I have never been a pessimist. I am, without doubt, an optimist, a glass-half-full person, and I cannot really put myself into the mindset of a pessimist. I have to say, though, that from my perspective it is difficult to see a pessimist being passionate about anything, unless he/she is passionate about being pessimistic.

My dad, for example, was passionate about his family, he was especially passionate about me, he was passionate about fishing, he was passionate about woodturning, and he was passionate about the music of brass bands. He was also passionate about mechanical things, particularly car engines, and our family cars were often in pieces; at times he even pulled our car engine apart to find out why it was running so well! Dad was a well-balanced man who always looked for the good in people and had faith in the future of our world. He was a man with a big heart, always ready to help his friends and neighbours with his practical mechanical expertise and in any other way that he could.

And that's one of the characteristics which we often notice in passionate people, and in optimists in general; they want to put their passions to work for the betterment of their fellow man, they want to help other people, and they want to make a positive difference in this world. Not so that they can be held up as examples and have people say, 'What a wonderful person!' but, in fact, quite the opposite, for in the main they are humble unassuming people who shun the limelight and just get on with helping other people whenever they can. They do it, in fact, because they cannot help themselves. It's part of who and what they are, part of their *raison d'être*.

Throughout this chapter the point is being made that Christians and non-Christians alike are often found living their lives passionately and with optimism. Christians do not have a monopoly on optimism, they are not the only ones to have passions which they live out in service to other people. And, with non-Christians of like mind we Christians share an enormous common-ground, and we should celebrate that. We must acknowledge, however, that there is a difference because as Christians we bring to the lives of other people something which the non-Christian cannot bring; we bring Jesus, we bring the love of God. In living our lives that way we are reflecting the love of God to the world as Jesus commanded us when he said:

> *Let your light shine before others, that they may see your good deeds and glorify your Father in heaven.*[1]

It should be said that the non-Christians who live their lives in that way are also reflecting the love of God to the world – they just don't know it!

I feel fortunate to have so many fine Christian friends and family who willingly give much of their time in the service of others. Space does not allow me to mention all of them here but let me tell you about just a few.

In Western Australia I have wonderful Christian friends, Rod and Sue, who are simply passionate about helping other people. Now, there is a passion that we could all emulate! Rod, and his wife Sue, spent many years in Northern Thailand building simple homes for refugees and tribal people near the Thai-Burma border. Now retired back in Perth, Rod is always the first to respond whenever he hears of anyone who is in need, particularly if it is a building or maintenance project, and Sue will always be right there beside him, digging holes, mixing concrete and hammering away.

Also living in Perth is my dear friend Ruth and I am truly blessed to count Ruth and her family among my good friends. Ruth, for many years struggled with deep clinical depression and even now she needs to manage it carefully. But Ruth changed her darkness into a passion by taking a Mental Health First Aid Facilitator's course and a Mental Health Counsellor's course. Now, through her writing and her public speaking, she brings hope and optimism into the lives of others who suffer from many forms of mental illness. Ruth and her husband, Simon, are also active in providing marriage-enrichment education to any churches or other organisations who have a need for that.

Another couple who are wonderful friends, John & Lexi, are passionate about caring for and giving their love to foster children. Hundreds of foster children, some short-term and some long-term, have passed through their care and been blessed by their love.

Then there are my good friends, lifelong friends, Don, and Heather, living in Sydney. Both are retired teachers. Don has, for many years, served as a volunteer chaplain in residential aged care facilities, an activity through which he brings love and blessings into the lives of many elderly and frail citizens. Meanwhile his wife, Heather, has found her passion, or one of them, in running free English language classes for non-English speaking immigrants.

And there's Luke, a friend in Brisbane, Queensland, whose passion is for prison ministry visiting prisons and meeting with the inmates in their communal recreation room, chatting with them and bringing a touch of humanity and friendship into their lives from the outside world.

My cousin, Lynette, is a Salvation Army officer assigned to be chaplain in the Sydney courts. Her passion is to serve God by supporting those going through the criminal court system, whether they be victims, accused perpetrators, or even police and investigators who witness many things that torment their minds; sometimes things that no person should have to witness.

And in Thailand, my friends Supote Ketudom and his wife Pimmart Ketudom have committed their lives to running a large safehouse for children who are at risk, particularly children who are at risk of being trafficked into forced labour and into the Thai sex industry.

The list could go on and on. God bless them all! We're all different, aren't we, and although we sometimes share passions with people of like mind, in many ways our passions reflect our skillsets, our interests in life, the circumstances of our backgrounds, our environmental upbringing, and in some cases a commitment to serve God in whatever way he presents to us. I wonder what your passions in life are. Whatever your passions, I thank God for them.

Me? I am passionate about writing and about speaking to others; about sharing with others the messages which I believe God has given me and entrusted me to pass on to others. Opportunities to speak to groups and gatherings do not come along all that often but the opportunity to speak with individuals is there every day, and I hope and pray that through my writing I am able to get the message out to a wider audience. I am also passionate about doing what I can to help end the scourge of human trafficking, especially the trafficking of children into forced labour or into the sex industry. To end that appalling and disgusting trade seems to be a daunting task, but I hope that by joining with organisations such as *Not For Sale* and *Stop the Traffik*[2], we can, with God's help, make a difference.

I have more personal passions, too, of course; I am a passionate browser of antique stores and I simply cannot pass one by. If it is a large antique shop, I can happily spend hours browsing and chatting with the proprietor, though I rarely buy anything. I am also passionate about researching our family history, a passion to which I was introduced by Heather who was mentioned earlier as the teacher of English to immigrants; this is a passion which I have discovered is absolutely addictive. I taught high school for more than 25 years and during that time I was passionate about passing on my knowledge to young and open minds, and watching my students grow and develop their own passions in life.

And, now in the autumn, if not the winter of my life, I am a passionate gardener. Although I have tended to move home numerous times over recent years, and for various reasons, gardening has remained a strong passion and at my current home I have many rose bushes, English and French lavenders, azaleas, camellias, wisterias and jacaranda trees. I have recently planted a magnolia tree and look forward to seeing it grow. I love the garden and there is little that I enjoy more than watching it burst into life at the beginning of spring; apart from the camellias which, of course, flower in winter. Now, I must confess that there are times when you might look at my garden and wonder where the passion has gone, why the garden appears so neglected and perhaps why there are so many of those plants in the wrong places (weeds). I would argue, however, that the passion is still there, and that it is only the availability of time and perhaps a few ageing bones which are not living up to their role in allowing me to fulfil my passion to the level of my own expectations, and yours.

But, and this is the important point, my gardening passion operates on two levels. You see, I have two gardens. One is the garden around my home, the one which sometimes looks a little un-kept. This is the garden where, amongst other plants, I have 38 rose bushes and I have to admit that sometimes I ask myself why anyone in their right mind would plant 38 rose bushes around their home; I inherited them when I bought my house. It is particularly at pruning time that I tend to ask that question. We will call this my literal garden.

But I also have a virtual garden, a vision in which the entire world is our garden, and I want to absolutely fill it with rose bushes. I like to call this our universal garden and we are all partners in this universal gardening project. Yes, all of us, including you, because every time you pray for the world or for your fellow man, every time you willingly lend a helping hand to your neighbour, every moment you spend visiting the sick, or prisoners, or those who are just lonely, every moment you spend helping a disabled child (disabled physically or mentally), you plant another rose in the garden. Every time you express an act of kindness and generosity to those in need, to the poor, to the hungry, to the homeless, to the downtrodden, you plant yet another rose. Every act of love and care to those who mourn, to those who are institutionalised in aged-care facilities, to the exploited and the vulnerable and to those who are marginalised by society, means another rose bush in the garden. Some people are gifted musicians, with a God-given passion for composing beautiful worship songs which lift-up and praise the name of Jesus and introduce others to the Lord of the world. Now, *that's* a big rose bush planted! Even a friendly smile to your neighbour, or to a stranger who you pass in the street, shines a little of God's love into this world, plants another rose, the rose garden grows, and the world is a better place because of it. And do you know something else that I love about this universal garden; God does the pruning, and the weeding! My task is just to plant.

Can you imagine how many rose bushes are being planted in our world? Luke is planting his roses in Queensland prisons. Supote and Pimmart are planting their roses in the lives of young at-risk children in Thailand, whilst John and Lexi plant their rose bushes in the lives of vulnerable foster children in Western Australia. Lynette plants her rose bushes in the lives of people who find themselves deeply involved in the traumatising environment of the criminal court system, both accused perpetrators and victims.

Ruth plants her rose bushes deep in some of the darkest places of the human experience, helping to bring light and hope to people suffering from mental illness, and to those who struggle to care for them. Don plants his roses in the lives of elderly and frail citizens in aged care facilities and Heather in the lives of the immigrant community. And Rod and Sue, they just plant their rose bushes wherever they go. It does not end there, of course. There are your rose bushes, and mine.

But let me tell you just a few things about this garden. I know that I have referred to it as 'my virtual garden' and as 'our universal garden' but I need to recant a little on that because, in fact, it is not our garden at all. It is God's Garden. We are given the enormous privilege of planting those roses, but when we plant them, they become his roses. That is why he does the pruning and the weeding, something for which I am eternally grateful. Our role is merely to plant God's roses, for his glory, so that his love can be seen to be reaching out into the darkest corners of this world, bringing his love and his grace to those in need. If you think it's your garden, if you think they are your rose bushes, if you think you are planting those roses for any purpose other than to glorify God, then you might as well be planting artificial flowers, cheap plastic imitations.

And a word of warning; one should not read into this a doctrine of salvation by works. We are saved by the grace of God through faith in Jesus Christ, and by nothing else. Planting a rose bush is not your key to salvation; planting a million rose bushes is not your key to salvation. As Christians we plant those rose bushes only because we love Jesus, our Lord, and we want others to see his love for the world. Of course, many non-Christians are also busy planting rose bushes which reflect their personal goodness and care for this world that we all live in, and in many cases those non-Christians put us Christians to shame. We must thank God for their efforts and join them in planting more and more rose bushes.

As we come to the end of this chapter let me say that I do believe that, in some way that I don't fully understand, God will use your rose bushes, and mine, when his Kingdom is revealed on earth. But don't take that to mean that through our efforts we are building the Kingdom of Heaven, or even that through our efforts we are hastening the day of the Kingdom. Building the Kingdom is God's job, and the timing of its fulfilment is known only to him. One day God will call a halt to our rose planting and say, 'You've done well, but I'll finish the garden from here.' In the meantime, that God wants to be doing it through his people, and particularly through his church, I have no doubt.

And now? It is the planting season. It is going on all over the world. Thousands upon thousands of people, indeed millions of people all over the world, are busy planting their own rose bushes in the lives of people that they touch in their local communities. Each of them is shining the love of God into this world and changing it for the better, and God is being glorified. And you ask me why I'm an optimist? Really?

1. Matthew 5:16
2. *https://www.notforsalecampaign.org/* and *www.stopthetraffik.org/*

Chapter 2
God's Grace is Enough

But life is not always easy. We all know that don't we? God never promised us a trouble-free life in this world, in fact just the opposite. There will be tough times – and that's a promise! I am not speaking of just a bad hair day now and then, not merely an occasional time when you don't feel on top of your game. This is not just the kids being kids and running you ragged, and the husband seemingly being unhelpful. This is much more than that. This is an iron-clad promise that in this world, in this life, you *are* going to have troubles, sometimes big troubles, sometimes huge troubles, sometimes troubles which you think you are never going to be able to endure. If you have escaped those troubles so far then count your blessings, and brace yourself, for they are coming!

'Whoa', I hear you say! 'What happened to the optimist of the previous chapter?' Well, he is still here, and the optimism has not waned, but it is complimented with a healthy sense of realism. Yes, complimented, because far from being mutually exclusive, optimism and realism are mutually complimentary, and both should be present in a well-balanced worldview. To live one's life as a realist without any sense of optimism or hope is to capitulate to circumstances which appear to be beyond our control and to risk descending into a deep sense of pessimism. To live exclusively as an optimist and to deny reality, on the other hand, is foolhardy and is akin to living in some kind of cloud-cuckoo land where everything appears to be perfect. The fact is that we live in exile, in a fallen world, in a world where things are not always perfect, and in a world where sometimes life hurts, and hurts deeply. It was not meant to be so.

In the 16th chapter of John's Gospel, Jesus is seen preparing his disciples for the fact that he will soon be taken from them. He is trying to prepare them for tough times ahead.

All this I have told you so that you will not fall away. They will put you out of the synagogue; in fact, the time is coming when anyone who kills you will think they are offering a service to God.[1]

Those prophetic words of Jesus were certainly actualised in the lives of the disciples and the apostles of the early church, many of whom, most, were martyred because of their faith. Chapter 16 of John's Gospel concludes with Jesus telling his disciples:

I have told you these things, so that in me you may have peace. In this world you will have trouble. But take heart! I have overcome the world.[2]

Look at those words, '*In this world you will have trouble.*' That is a promise! Jesus was not saying 'Maybe you will have tough days now and then', or 'maybe you will have troubles' but rather 'you *will* have trouble.' It is definite! It is also something of an understatement. Jesus was not talking about an occasional day when a few things go wrong, he was speaking huge troubles, possibly even life and death.

At this point a long list, perhaps an infinite list, could be drawn up of the kinds of huge troubles which can afflict us in this fallen world. But the list is not necessary because all of us have seen them, and you may have endured some of them. Of course, you are not the only person to have faced those troubles, others face similar or identical troubles; financial troubles, domestic violence, failing marriages, unfaithfulness and souring relationships, betrayal, exploitation, sexual and psychological abuse, slander and untrue defamations, the death of someone who is very dear to you. None of us is exempt from hurt and suffering; Christians and non-Christians alike are subject to suffering and troubles in this fallen world. Tears are tears whether they flow from Christian eyes or non-Christian eyes; one thing which we all have in common is that we all know what it means to hurt, all too often.

Yes, other people go through the same troubles that you and I endure, sometimes worse troubles, but when it happens to you, it's yours. It is unique to you. You own it! It hits you in the gut and the reality of it can swamp your optimism. The question is, how are you going to cope with it? What are you going to do about it? Will your faith falter? Will you 'fall away', in Jesus' words?

The journey of life is not always easy. Psalm 84 mentions traveling through the 'Valley of Baka'.[3] As far as we know, the Valley of Baka was not a geographic place on the map, though it is possible that it may once have been some hot desert valley devoid of water. More likely, however, is that the psalmist was using the term figuratively because it translates as 'Valley of Tears'. Now, *that* place exists! I have been there several times. Perhaps you, too, have been there. Perhaps you are there now. And, if you have been there, was your faith tested, did your faith falter, did you 'fall away'? It is okay to answer 'yes'. I, too, must answer 'yes' to all those questions, but I am here to tell you that there is a way back.

The story that I am about to tell you will be painful for me to write. Although I have spoken to people about some aspects of this experience, I have never told the entire story, either in spoken word or in writing. Perhaps I need to do so.

Early in 2013 I chose to relocate from my home in Perth to the city of Melbourne. For those who might be unfamiliar with the geography of Australia, that meant moving three and a half thousand kilometres, right across the country, from the west coast to the east. As I prepared to make the move, I realised that the one thing that I was going to miss more than any other was the church family at the church where I had been worshiping for some years. I knew that I was going to miss the people in that church community and their love for me which I had known over the time that I had been there. But I thought 'It'll be all right. I will be able to get established at another church. I'll be able to cope with this.'

It was a big move and I really had two reasons for making the move; firstly, there were family considerations. Ours was a small family, my father having passed-away many years ago meant that there was just me, my elderly and frail mother, and Leanne, my only sibling. Leanne had suffered serious illnesses on and off over the years and I just felt that I wanted and needed to be closer to both my mother and my sister. Neither of them lived in Melbourne, they both lived in country towns some distance from Melbourne, but at least I would be on the right side of the country.

My second reason for making the move was that I just love Melbourne city. I love its rich multiculturalism, I love its heritage architecture, I love the gardens and parks, the trams, the galleries, museums, and theatres, the bayside beaches and the sporting events, especially my beloved AFL football. Melbourne is certainly my most favoured Australian state capital. So, I made the move. I bought a penthouse apartment (13th floor) in a beautiful hi-rise building on Melbourne's premier boulevard, St Kilda Rd, with a wonderful view across Albert Park Lake to the city skyline, and I loved it there. Trams at my front door and a seven-minute ride into the vibrant downtown area of central Melbourne, fifteen minutes by tram to Australia's greatest sporting stadium, a ten-minute drive to the bay beaches, and coffee shops everywhere! I should mention that I am addicted to coffee, and there is no doubt that Melbourne is the coffee-capital of Australia, perhaps of the world. Several months passed; I had not got around to establishing myself at a local church, but I was about to do that. Life was good, and then my sister got sick – very sick.

Leanne had suffered from a mysterious and debilitating illness on and off over the years. It seemed that it would disappear for a couple of years but then would reappear for perhaps 6 or 12 months. It was a serious illness which attacked her nervous system causing her to lose much of the control of her limbs, her bladder, and bowels. It also caused great abdominal pain and caused her body to tremble and convulse quite violently. At times, with all my strength I could not hold her. Doctors were absolutely mystified by the illness, unable to diagnose a cause, and could only hope each time it disappeared that it would not recur. But, of course, it did recur and when it recurred in mid-2013 it struck with a much greater vengeance.

Leanne lived with her family, her husband and two daughters in their 20s, in a regional centre about three hours' drive north of Melbourne and with the local doctors bereft of ideas the family decided that I should take Leanne to live with me in the Melbourne apartment whilst we tried to find a Melbourne based doctor who might be able to help.

Over the next several months I took her to every major hospital in Melbourne, and I took her to every doctor who would see us, all to no avail. Leanne's condition continued to rapidly deteriorate in a downward spiral and the city doctors really had no more to offer than had the country doctors. Some doctors suggested that it was a mental illness, and that Leanne should seek psychiatric help, a suggestion which I encouraged Leanne to explore but one which she flatly refused to consider. Rightly or wrongly, she was convinced that it was a purely physical illness. Some doctors recognised the physical deterioration, but none were able to pin it down to a firm diagnosis. The closest we came to a physical diagnosis were a couple of doctors who suggested that it 'might be porphyria'. Porphyria is a rare disease, difficult to diagnose and impossible to cure, with symptoms which include severe abdominal pain, chest pain, violent body tremors, vomiting, confusion, constipation, diarrhoea, fever, high blood pressure and high heart rate. Most of Leanne's symptoms fitted with that. Porphyria can also, over time, adversely affect the nervous system and mental capacity. It can, at its worst, end with the patient becoming insane. Some readers may have seen the movie *The Madness of King George*' (George III of England). Some modern-day historians believe that George was suffering from porphyria.

What I observed living in the apartment with my sister were both severe physical symptoms as well as mental capacity deterioration. Whether it was a mental illness driving physical symptoms, or whether it was a physical illness driving mental instability, I did not know. I still don't know. Leanne herself refused to entertain any suggestion that it was a mental illness. What I do know is that day by day, sometimes hour by hour, she deteriorated both physically and emotionally/mentally.

It was, I believe, a symptom of her illness that she became totally obsessed with her condition. She researched it endlessly on the internet to the point that she knew much more than many of the doctors we saw which, of course, did nothing to endear her to them. And whether in the apartment or in the car, and wherever I took her, she wanted to talk about her illness constantly, and I do mean constantly; 24/7. I calculated that during the eight months that Leanne lived in the apartment we would not have had more than a total of 20 minutes conversation about any other subject. That is a total of 20 minutes over eight months! And that is where I started to fail; that constant obsession with discussing the illness over and over again was like being trapped in a revolving door. It was consuming me and driving me towards a complete breakdown. I became constantly frustrated, I became angry with my sister, I refused to talk to her about the illness, and sometimes I went to my room and locked the door to get away from it.

Every day I spent hours in my room praying for healing, praying that we would find a doctor who could help, and it seemed that my prayers were being ignored. I recalled the words of Job; 'I cry out to you, O God', Job said, 'but you do not answer'.[4] I could relate to that! At times I screamed at God, telling him that he didn't care, telling him that Leanne was a strong Christian who loved the Lord, that she was one of his people, that he was being utterly cruel to put one of his children through such suffering. I even, at times, screamed at God telling him that he didn't exist, which is a pretty stupid thing to do when you consider the logic of screaming at someone who you believe doesn't exist, but it did show my mental state and the depths of my despair. After about six months, when it became apparent to me that God was not going to heal my sister, I changed the focus of my prayers and prayed "Lord, just give her a sense of peace and a calm mind. Is that too much to ask?"

Apparently, it was too much to ask because that did not happen either; her mental condition continued to spiral downwards and out of control.

A Christian friend, recognising my own deteriorating condition, gave me a book to read. Although I acknowledge that giving me that book was an act of Christian love, I will not tell you the title of the book because I am going to be quite disparaging about it. It was a book along the lines of how to lean on God when you are suffering, and I read about half of it before I threw it in the trash can. It seemed, to me, to be a book of clichés and empty platitudes and I found myself asking 'Has this guy, the author, ever really suffered as I am suffering now? How can he serve up this trash to people who are living through such intense suffering?'

Both of us, my sister and I, were on a terrible spiral into the abyss, both physically and mentally. In addition to that, I knew that my faith had faltered, that it had been severely tested. At times I believed that I had failed that test, and perhaps I had. If I had not turned my back on God, then I was close to it. God seemed not to exist. Leanne was oblivious to what her illness and her obsession with it was doing to me. She is not to blame for that, it was the illness, but I too was sinking deeper into despair, perhaps into my own mental illness. It could not go on, but it did go on, and on, and on.

Around 6am on the morning of 13th March 2014 I was awakened by the persistent and urgent knocking on the front door of my apartment. I climbed out of bed, pulled on a gown, and went to answer the door where I was confronted by a large contingent of police officers. I must have stared at them blankly until the senior officer asked my name. I told him my name and he then asked whether I was the owner of the apartment. When I confirmed that I was the owner, he said to me 'We are here because on the pavement at ground level, under your balcony, there is the body of a deceased woman. We believe that she is from this apartment.'

What? **What!**

I cannot be sure what happened next. I think he took hold of my arm, and had he not done so I suspect I would have fallen. I felt my stomach drop, like an elevator in free-fall, down, down, down, until it smashed into the basement and my knees buckled. Somehow, I got to one of the couches in the living room and fell into it for a few moments whilst the police officers waited for me to recover a little from the shock.

After a few moments, they asked me to show them my sister's room. I led them to the room, but they would not allow me to open the door. They insisted on opening the door themselves, very carefully, and it seemed they were intent on not smudging any fingerprints which might have been on the door handle. The bed had been slept in, but the room was empty. We repeated the same procedure at the bathroom door – empty. The police inspected my bedroom too. I turned to the large glass sliding doors leading out onto the balcony, but they stood in front of me and stopped me. I was told that I would not be allowed on the balcony until after the balcony railings had been examined for fingerprints, and the senior officer said to me 'And believe me, you do not want to look over that balcony!'

The next couple of hours were pretty much a blur. I had to make a statement about what I knew, and when I was finger-printed I realised that they were considering the possibility that I may have thrown my sister off the balcony. They asked a lot of questions; When did you last see her? What was she wearing? What was said? What was her demeanour last night? I remember screaming at them; 'She was sick! She was bloody sick!' There was an empty coffee cup on the kitchen bench – not mine. It too, was examined and fingerprints taken. There was no note.

Eventually, it seemed that they concluded that I had not been involved in Leanne's death. Leanne's fingerprints on the balcony railing indicated that she had climbed over the railing and had held on there from the other side before letting go and falling to her death. The fingerprints were noticeably clear, not smudged, a sign which the police told me was an indication that there had been no struggle. It was at that point that I was asked to go down to ground level and to identify the body; without doubt the hardest thing that I have ever had to do. The area at ground level below my balcony was a car parking area, and there was a low vertical concrete wall to divide the lanes of traffic, about a metre high and maybe 20cm wide. When Leanne fell, her body fell onto that wall and, on impact, her body was broken into two pieces, at the waist. I was only shown the top section of the body, the upper torso and face. It was enough. In a daze I just nodded and scribbled my signature on their identity release papers. I noticed that there were some workmen there with a large fire hose, washing away a large amount of blood, washing away my sister.

The senior policeman and a policewoman took me back upstairs to the apartment, sat me down, got me a glass of water, and said 'Are you all right?' Am I all right? What a question! What did they expect me to say? I just closed my eyes and nodded. They said something about leaving some business cards on the kitchen bench, their own cards and the cards of counselling services, then they left, and I was alone in an empty apartment. And I, too, was empty; totally drained physically, emotionally, and spiritually. I was a non-person surrounded by silence and a total void. Nothing seemed to exist, and I am not even sure that I was aware that I, myself, was still real, that I existed.

'In this world you will have trouble.' Tell me about it!

I sat there lost in absolute nothingness for a few hours. I was delaying the next awful task, that of telling the awful news to Leanne's daughters. I could not tell them that news on the telephone, so finally I got in my car, drove the three hours to the town where they lived, and had to deliver that dreadful news to those who loved her.

I knew that I had to reach out to get some help for myself. Incapable of praying for myself I called the church which I had attended back in Perth and spoke to the senior pastor, a good friend, asking for prayer support. But then I just retreated into myself and sat there alone, for days, not eating, not bathing, not thinking, certainly not praying. Although I did not realise it at the time, calling my pastor friend at that church was a turning point for me. That church sprang into action, holding special prayer sessions in church services, in small groups and in individual homes. I was inundated with messages of love and the church made a very practical gift to me – the church leadership sent my best friends, Rod and Sue, mentioned in the previous chapter, right across the country, to be with me at that terrible time. Rod and Sue were on the first flight out of Perth, and when they arrived, they held me and told me that they had come to be with me for as long as I needed them. I wept. For the first time since my sister's death, I wept.

I did have a few visitors during those early days when I was deep in the depths of despair – one Christian couple who told me that Leanne's medical condition had not improved because her faith had not been strong enough. I asked them to leave, closed the door behind them, and then I metaphorically tossed them into the trash can along with the book of empty platitudes.

At the funeral service, another man told me that suicide is a sin and that, because of the nature of the sin, it is a sin which one can never confess, a sin of which one can never repent. The implication was that suicide is an unforgiveable sin, that when a Christian takes his or her own life, that person is rejected by God. I said 'thank you for coming' then I walked away from him and he too, metaphorically, joined the book of empty platitudes in the trash can.

Sometime soon after the funeral I travelled to Perth to stay with Rod and Sue for a few weeks. I particularly wanted to be at that church, to be surrounded by their love, and to thank them. And it was good for me. I am sure that going there was part of

God's plan for me because that is where God made a start, yes, a very small start, to refresh my spirit and to restore my faith.

I would dearly love to believe that, in the end, my faith was strong enough to get me through that crisis, but I know that was not the case. I am reminded of the events recorded in John's gospel when many of Jesus' followers turned away and no longer followed him. At this, Jesus turned to the twelve disciples and asked, 'Will you, also, leave me?' Simon Peter answered saying 'Lord, where else can we go?'[5] That's how I felt. I had screamed at God and told him that he didn't exist, I too had left him, but where else could I go? I turned to that church in Perth in an act of desperation because I had nowhere else to go. I seemed incapable of reaching out to Jesus myself, but I knew that the people in that church would reach out to him for me.

It has been a long journey back from the abyss. I had two years of suicide bereavement counselling. It helped, but it didn't, if you know what I mean. I found that I could not continue to live in that apartment, so I sold it and moved interstate to the Hunter Valley, to be closer to extended family who love me and who care for me. The guilt remains – that is the biggest load that I carry. My thoughts are cyclic – if I had not moved from Perth to Melbourne then Leanne would not have been there in Melbourne. If I had not bought a penthouse apartment in a hi-rise building, she would not have been there on the top floor. I should have been more patient with her, I should have listened more, I should have talked to her more. Those 'should have' things still hold me down in a sense of failure and of guilt. I should have made sure that she knew how much I loved her. Instead, I live with the awful feeling that she died thinking that she was all alone, that I did not love her.

A couple of years after Leanne's death I was back in her hometown, visiting my two nieces, Leanne's daughters. Leanne's husband, Tom, had also passed-away in the intervening period. I think he never got over Leanne's tragic death. During that visit I had coffee in a café with Michelle, one of Leanne's closest friends.

Michelle could see, just by looking at me, that I was still carrying that burden of guilt. She just reached out and put her hand on my hand, and said to me 'Give it to God, Ian. Give it to God.' I am trying to do that, but it is easier said than done; I am trying, and I think my state of mind is improving, but it is a long way back. It is only now, almost 7 years since Leanne's death, that I am beginning to put my pain into perspective and to find some hope. If I found little hope during the suffering of that terrible time, I am beginning to find hope beyond the suffering.

That has been a long story, but it has been a cathartic release for me to get it down on paper. I beg your indulgence. I hope and pray that you will not be asked to experience such deep and painful troubles, but I do know, and you know, that in this world you will have troubles of your own. There is almost no limit to the kind of troubles which we can encounter in this world; the death of a child or another loved one, unjust and false defamation, rumours and innuendos, financial failure and bankruptcy, unfair dismissal by an employer, wayward and troubled teenage children, relationship breakdowns, the awful words from a long-term spouse 'I don't love you anymore. I'm leaving', addictions, and any number of other troubles which can beset us. I have no doubt that all readers will have encountered some of those problems. Some readers may be going through such troubles as you read this book.

I will not offer you those clichés and empty platitudes. Many would expect that in a Christian book that is what I should do, but I cannot do that. I cannot tell you that God will never allow you to face anything which you cannot endure. Indeed, when people make that claim it is a misrepresentation of Scripture for its basis is in Paul's first letter to the church at Corinth in which he wrote:

> *And God is faithful; he will not let you be tempted beyond what you can bear.*[6]

This verse comes in the middle of a chapter concerning being tempted to sin and Paul is saying that God will not allow you to be tempted to sin, beyond which you are able to resist. It has nothing to do with suffering and Paul was not saying that God will not allow you to suffer affliction beyond which you can endure. Clearly, that is not the case and Leanne is evident proof of that for she was certainly unable to endure the pain and mental anguish inflicted upon her. I cannot tell you that if you just turn to God in prayer, that God will answer your prayers and that your suffering will end. That does not always happen – it does sometimes, but it is not a guaranteed promise. We all know of ardent and faithful prayers by God's people which have seemingly been unanswered, and my own constant prayers over that eight-month period are example of that.

So, where is God when life hurts? Why do bad things happen to good people, to God's people? I have heard Christian friends say that we just don't have the answer to that question, but I think that we do, and I think the answer is quite simple. Bad things happen to good people because we live in a fallen world, a world of our own making. It was not meant to be so, but we chose to live in this fallen world when, through our sin and the sin of all mankind, we separated ourselves from the perfect world which God had created. That is why Jesus said, 'In *this world* you will have trouble.' We may wish that it were not so, but God, too, wishes that it were not so. God loves us with a love beyond description and it pains him, it agonises him, that we must live in this fallen world and suffer the ills of this fallen world.

So, again, where is God when life hurts? God is there with us, right alongside us, sharing in our despair, sharing in our pain, sharing in our suffering. Being the flawed humans that we are, we often fail to recognise that God is there with us. We tend to look inwards, to be self-absorbed and self-focused, to be self-obsessed with our own suffering, and so we may think that we are alone during those difficult times. That was certainly the case for me during Leanne's illness, her death, and beyond. But we are not alone, our God is the God of compassion and that very word, compassion, means that God suffers with us. The word 'compassion' comes from the Latin, *cumpassio*, a compound of two Latin words, *passio* meaning 'to suffer', and *cum* meaning 'with'. In those dark times, whether we realise it or not, our God is right there, suffering alongside us and carrying us through the trough.

Despite the sadness of Leanne's story, this book sets out to be a book of hope and of encouragement. I remain an optimist; I look to the future with optimism and with a healthy sense of reality. And Jesus, too, wanted to encourage us; he wanted us to be realists and at the same time he wanted to encourage us to be optimists. The realism was expressed in his words 'In this life you will have trouble.' The encouragement came in the very next words, 'But take heart! I have overcome the world'.[7] The glass is half full – more than half full.

I enjoy reading, time and time again, the first letter of the apostle Peter in the New Testament. I've asked myself 'is this the same rambunctious and hot-headed Peter that we read about in the Gospels?' and if some renowned biblical scholars were to say 'No, this is another Peter' then I could easily be led to believe that. For in-fact, this is not the same Peter; this is not even the Peter who on the day of Pentecost stood up and preached 'Jesus Christ is alive!'; this is Peter the older more mature Peter, now probably too old to take his boat out, this is the gentle Old Fisherman expressing the wisdom that can only come through the gift of the Holy Spirit. Peter was writing to Christians spread throughout the known world of Asia Minor and he was writing to them as they tried to endure the sufferings and persecutions being imposed upon them by the mad Emperor Nero. Those people lived in fear, very real fear, that their blood, like the blood of many other Christians before them, would soak the ground of the Colosseum for Nero's entertainment, or that they might be made human torches to light the streets of Rome.

And the Old Fisherman did not tell those fellow Christians to draw their swords and to fight back, as the younger impetuous Peter may have done, indeed as the younger Peter himself had done in Gethsemane, but neither did he offer them those empty platitudes. He didn't try to convince them that everything would be all right, but he tried to encourage them to look ever towards Jesus Christ, and to show them that through knowing that the God of compassion was present in that persecution with them that they could be filled with his grace and peace. This letter is a simple reassurance that though the journey of faith through this life may be difficult and even life-threatening, our God walks that path with us. No promises that Nero's reign of terror would soon end, no promises of better days ahead, no reassurances that everything would work out all right, no exhortations to 'just hang in there', just the promise of Christ's peace and grace in the face of terrible persecution. Peter had heard, first-hand from the Lord's mouth, *'In this world you will have trouble. But take heart, I have overcome the world!'* and now here he was, the Old Fisherman, writing to those who were suffering the worst persecution imaginable to say to them 'Take heart! God's grace is enough for you'.

One of my favourite books, and a book that I have read so many times that I fear I have almost worn the print off the page, is Charles Swindoll's lovely book, *Laugh Again – Hope Again; Two Books to Inspire a Joy-Filled Life*. It is a book that I can highly recommend to those who struggle to find hope in the face of adversity (for details see the bibliography). As the sub-title suggests, it is two books in one, and in the second of those books, *Hope Again*, under a chapter which Swindoll has called *Hope Beyond Suffering*, he has written:

'Suffering comes in many forms and degrees, but his grace is always there to carry us beyond it. I've lived long enough and endured a sufficient number of trials to say without hesitation that only Christ's perspective can replace our resentment with rejoicing. Jesus is the central piece of suffering's puzzle. If we fit him into place, the rest of the puzzle, no matter how complex and enigmatic, begins to make sense.'[8]

I find that true in my own life. I sometimes wonder how those who do not know Jesus manage to cope with the trials and sufferings they encounter in this life. In truth, it is not something that I should find myself wondering about – I really should know because I spent the first fifty-seven years of my life living like that. It is just that knowing Jesus has made such an immense change in my life, and in my attitude towards suffering, that I now find it difficult to remember living like that.

There was a time, some years before the death of my sister, when I was living in Western Australia and even then, Leanne was periodically ill. On one such occasion when she had been ill for several months, I found myself in a state of despair because of her illness. I felt totally helpless because I was some three and a half thousand kilometres away but then, even if I had been with her, I would have been at a loss to know what I could do to help her. I remember that on a Saturday morning I was feeling particularly low and helpless, burdened with a sense of enormous frustration and, on that morning, I just felt that I had to get out and go somewhere in the car. I needed to get out and get some fresh air and, although I didn't realise it when I set out, I needed to find a place where I could just sit down and talk with God. And so, I set out in the car, not knowing where I was going. Without knowing the reason, I took my Bible with me.

If you are driving out of Perth you have a choice; north, south, or east. If you head west, you'll soon be in the Indian Ocean. For no particular reason, I decided to head east and as I drove, I felt myself being prompted by the Holy Spirit – 'Go to Lake Leschenaultia.' I'd been there before, at least thirty years earlier I had done a little unsuccessful fishing there, but it was so long since I had been there that I had to stop at a gas station to ask the way. Still uncertain about why I was going to the lake I drove on and as I did so I tried to recall in my mind a picture of the lake as I remembered it. I remembered that there was a small café there, so I thought I would be able to get a coffee and maybe lunch at some point.

I like to listen to music as I drive, so I shuffled through the menu on the car's audio system and stopped on an album by Chris

Tomlin. I sang along with several of the worship songs on the album, and then the next song really jumped out at me and spoke to me; *'Your Grace Is Enough.'* Of course, I had heard the song before, I had even sung it in congregational singing, but I had never before actually taken much notice of the words that I had sung. But there was Chris Tomlin calling on God to remember his people, to remember his promise, to remember his children and praising God by singing 'Your grace is enough.' It prompted me to pray, even as I was driving, to remind God of his promises, to remind him that my sister loved the Lord and that she was a child of God, and it encouraged me to call on God to remember her in her present illness. That song said to me that whatever may happen, God's grace is enough. I was not totally sure that I believed it, but I listened to that song several times before arriving at the lake.

Well, the lake was deserted, the café was closed. I guess there was no reason to have been surprised, after all it was mid-winter. But I found a log, a fallen tree, to sit on in the sunshine. I prayed briefly, telling God that I really did not know why I was there, then I looked at the Bible in my hands; what would I read? I really had no idea what to read so I decided to start with a few of my favourite verses of Scripture, from the book of Jeremiah.

> *I have loved you with an everlasting love, I have drawn you with loving kindness. I will build you up again and you will be rebuilt, O virgin Israel. Again, you will take up your tambourines and go out to dance with the joyful.*[9]

Again, I prayed, and again I reminded God about his promise, contained in those words, and then the Holy Spirit was nudging me, prompting me, 'read Psalm 23'. As I started to read that psalm, I read '*He leads me beside still waters*'[10] and I looked out at the lake; it was *perfectly still*, not a ripple, it was like glass, and I knew then that God had led me to that place, and I cried. I thanked God for bringing me to that place, I thanked him for being there with me; in my own way I was rejoicing in that time of sadness. And then I read on, '*He restores my soul*', much the same message as the Jeremiah verses, '*I will build you up again.*'[11] I stayed there about four hours, mostly praying, re-reading and pondering Psalm 23. I went for a walk at one stage and then back to the log for more prayer and reflection. I had come to love that log – it was a place where I felt embraced by warmth. I was grateful to have the place to myself. Well, God and I had the place to ourselves. I left the lake about 4pm. It was getting cold by then, so I headed home.

There is a sequel to that story – the next night, Sunday night, after a time of prayer, I listened again to Chris Tomlin's song *Your Grace Is Enough*. I am quite sure that many readers will know how sometimes words in a song slip by without actually registering. Sometimes words can be hard to pick up clearly. I sat in my dark living room, all the lights off, listening to this song and suddenly I heard something that I had not heard before. I thought 'Did he really sing that?' I replayed it and, 'Yes, I think he did sing that'. I hurried to the computer and pulled up the lyrics on the internet and, YES, those words were there. 'You lead us by still waters.' I sat there in the dark, crying and shaking my head.

There is absolutely no doubt in my mind that I was led to that lake on that Saturday morning by the Holy Spirit. I have absolutely no doubt that it was the Spirit who guided me in turning to the specific scriptures that I read there on that log. And I have absolutely no doubt that Chris Tomlin's song was part of the gift of grace which God gave to me at that time of need. It didn't resolve our troubles, Leanne wasn't restored to health and I still didn't know what I could do to help her, but it did encourage me to be reminded that God was there suffering with us and that, for that day, God's Grace was enough.

We are all different people and because of that the troubles which we must endure are also different. Suffering comes in many shades and something which you might take in your stride might hit me hard and have me questioning whether I am ever going to get through it. But no matter what the nature of the troubles and sorrows which we might be experiencing at any given time, God's grace is tailor-made for our needs. Sometimes, blinded by our suffering, we fail to see God's grace, but that is not to say that it is not there. Although there have been times when I have been so insular in my suffering that I have failed to see his grace, I do know deep within myself that his grace is always there to carry us through the suffering and pain. God's grace is always enough for today. What I must learn to do is to seek his grace again tomorrow.

All followers of Jesus Christ believe in their hearts that Jesus certainly has overcome the world. We believe that through the power of God he was raised from the dead, defeating the power of death, the ultimate manifestation of the evil one's power. And now God, in his grace, extends that victory to us. This fallen world in which we live is gradually being restored to its original and perfect state, in some small measure by those rose bushes that we plant, but more definitively by the grace and the power of a God who is determined to rescue his good creation from the bondage of sin with which we have enslaved it, and to create a new heavens and a new earth where the glory of God will be poured out of the New Jerusalem to fill the whole earth.

I look forward to that day immensely. I cannot wait! But in the meantime, I reflect upon the fact that so far in this life I have experienced two of those very painful journeys through the Valley of Baka. This is not the place to tell you of the second such journey. I will share that in a later chapter but suffice to say here that it was dark, and that it lasted for several years. Looking back on it, I know that God was suffering with me, though I might not have fully realised it at the time.

Some years before I visited the lake on that Saturday morning, I had come across those words in the book of Jeremiah which I read by the lake that day. Those few verses would become very dear to me – verses which would sustain me, verses which I would hold onto for dear life. My cousin, Lynette, embroidered those verses on a cushion for me (thank you Cuz!) and I well remember many despairing nights when I just sat in my living room, in the dark, crying, with that cushion clutched close against my chest. I know that those words were a specific promise from God to the ancient Israelites suffering during their time in exile in Babylon, but I hold those words as a promise for me too:

> *I have loved you with an everlasting love, I have drawn you with loving kindness. I will build you up again and you will be rebuilt, O virgin Israel. Again, you will take up your tambourines and go out to dance with the joyful.*[12]

God cares about us, he loves us greatly, and he shares in our suffering. I am here to tell you that from the deepest and darkest hole, there is a path that lifts us out of that trough and towards the next peak. I am slowly being rebuilt, and I need to start taking tambourine lessons. I am a work in progress. We are all works in progress.

1. John 16:1-2
2. John 16:33
3. Psalm 84:6
4. Job 30:20
5. John 6:68
6. 1 Corinthians 10:13
7. John 16:33
8. Swindoll, Charles R. *Hope Again*, in chapter 2, *Hope Beyond Suffering*
9. Jeremiah 31:3-4
10. Psalm 23:2
11. Jeremiah op-cit
12. Ibid.

Chapter 3
This too shall pass

The saying, 'This too shall pass' is often attributed to the Bible, but those words are not found in the Bible. Similar sentiments are indeed found in the Bible, but the actual use of those precise words is thought to have originated, as far as we know, in the writings of medieval Sufi (Persian) poets. We do find that God had expressed similar sentiments through his prophet Jerimiah, in Jerimiah's letter to the exiles in Babylon, parts which we will look at shortly. In the New Testament, too, the apostle Paul came close to expressing the same sentiments when he wrote to the church at Corinth:

For our present troubles are small and won't last very long. Yet they produce for us a glory that vastly outweighs them and will last forever. So, we don't look at the troubles we can see now; rather, we fix our gaze on things that cannot be seen. For the things we see now will soon be gone, but the things we cannot see will last forever.[1]

Regardless of the origin of the words, 'This too shall pass' is today an adage known throughout the world as an encouraging expression of hope, reflecting on the temporal nature of the human condition.

The prophet Jeremiah, it seems to me, gets a lot of bad press. He is often spoken of as the 'Prophet of Doom.' Indeed, in our culture when talking of someone who often brings bad news we are sometimes inclined say 'He's a real Jeremiah!' The real Jeremiah was, of course, despised by the Jewish people because he was a persistent bearer of bad-news-prophecies. Jeremiah constantly prophesised that unless the people of Judah repented of their sins and turned to God, then God's judgement would be unleashed upon them in the most disastrous ways. Nobody likes bad news, especially when there is an alternative, and the false prophets of the day were providing that alternative, telling the people not to worry and that everything would be fine. It is difficult to ignore the parallels with our own society today.

And yet, the book of Jeremiah in the Old Testament is one of my favourite books in the Bible. Despite the doom and gloom prophecies which Jeremiah delivered to the people of Judah in his day, and which can be applied to our society today, one of the things that I really enjoy about his prophecy is the clarity of his language. I have been a translator and a language teacher for almost 50 years, so clarity of language is important to me. Rarely do we need to struggle with interpreting obscure analogies in Jeremiah's prophecy as is often the case with the writings of the other prophets. Jeremiah spells it out just the way it is, in plain and unambiguous language. You can ignore the message, but you cannot claim not to have understood it. No doubt that is part of the reason he was so vehemently disliked by the rulers and people of Judah during his time.

And, sprinkled in with those bad-news-prophecies we find God's message seasoned with many uplifting and encouraging verses. None more so, for me, than those words used at the end of the previous chapter; *'I have loved you with an everlasting love.'*[2] I still hold onto those words closely.

Being a prophet in Jeremiah's time was certainly a tough gig. God had been speaking through his prophets for well over a hundred years, confronting the Jewish people with their sin and calling on them to repent and thereby avoid the impending disaster of God's judgment upon them. A hundred years before Jeremiah, the prophet Isaiah had been prophesizing the conquest of Judah by the Babylonians and had continually called on the people to repent even though God, himself, knew that they would not repent.

When Jeremiah was delivering God's message to the people of the southern kingdom of Judah, the northern kingdom of Israel had already suffered conquest at the hands of the Assyrians who commenced taking captive Israelites to Assyria in around 740BC.

The capital of the northern kingdom, Samaria, fell to the Assyrian army in 722BC. But for the people of the southern kingdom of Judah, and its capital Jerusalem, conquest would come at the hands of the even more ruthless Babylonians who destroyed Jerusalem in 597BC and carried off many thousands of people from Jerusalem to exile in Babylon. Jeremiah prophesised that the Babylonian exile would last precisely seventy years. It did.

What is clear from the book of Jeremiah is the longsuffering patience of God. Jeremiah had been appealing to the people of Judah for decades that they should change their ways and turn back to God to avoid destruction and exile. In fact, Isaiah had prophesied 100 years earlier that they would be defeated by the Babylonians and taken into exile if they did not repent of their wickedness.[3] But, of course, the people of Judah did not repent, as God knew would be the case, and God's judgment was ultimately visited upon them.

I do believe, however, that having to bring that punishment upon his people must have greatly pained and grieved God. For hundreds of years, he had pleaded with them to repent so that this conquest and exile could be avoided, and I believe that it broke his heart when, ultimately, the punishment had to be delivered. Our God is unchanging, from time eternal to time eternal; he is the God of compassion today and he was the God of compassion in Jeremiah's time. He was there, with the exiles, suffering alongside them in Babylon.

And do you see the parallels here? Because of our sin, from the time of the fall until the present day all of mankind has been exiled from God's kingdom and his heart is broken because of that separation. But, as we have seen, Jesus wanted us to 'take heart', to be optimistic and when he said to us 'Take heart! I have overcome the world'[4] I believe that he was, in effect, saying to us 'Okay, you are not in the place where you should be, you are exiled here in this fallen world where you will have troubles, but be positive because I have it under control. This too shall pass.'

In the 29th chapter of the book bearing his name, Jeremiah writes a letter from Jerusalem to the exiles in Babylon.[5] In that letter Jeremiah urges them to reconcile themselves to their captivity, to make a life for themselves there, after all they are going to be there for 70 years and only their children and their grandchildren were ever going to return to Jerusalem. And so, Jeremiah writes:

> *This is what the* LORD *Almighty, the God of Israel, says to all those I carried into exile from Jerusalem to Babylon: 'Build houses and settle down; plant gardens and eat what you produce. Marry and have sons and daughters; find wives for your sons and give your daughters in marriage, so that they too may have sons and daughters. Increase in number there; do not decrease. Also, seek the peace and prosperity of the city to which I have carried you into exile. Pray to the* LORD *for it, because if it prospers, you too will prosper.'*[6]

That sounds very much to me that, through his prophet Jeremiah, God was sending a message of hope and of encouragement to those exiles in their pain and suffering.

I must clarify one other verse in this letter. It is a very well-known verse, which is often interpreted as a beautiful promise of God:

> *For I know the plans I have for you, declares the* LORD, *plans to prosper you and not to harm you, plans to give you hope and a future.*[7]

Beautiful though it is, I think that many Christians today simply think 'well, that's nice – I'll just tuck that away as one of those nice things that God says to us'. But to the exiles in Babylon this was a vital promise, assuring the exiles that God had not forgotten them, that he would deliver them from exile. And, just like the exiles in Babylon, we are equally justified in taking that promise as being applicable to us for, of course, we too are exiles.

And we know that God *does* have good plans for us, He *does* want to prosper us, He *does* want to give us hope and a future. I think the translation of the King James Version might capture the intent a little more accurately:

> *For I know the thoughts that I think toward you, saith the LORD, thoughts of peace, and not of evil, to give you an expected end.*[8]

Those last words of the King James translation nail it for me; *'to give you an expected end.'* I think this is a message of encouragement to the captives in Babylon. I think that God is saying 'Don't despair. I love you and I have not forgotten you. There is an end in sight. This time of exile, too, shall pass.'

God says the same to us, today, in this fallen world. 'Build houses and settle down, for you are going to be there for some time. Plant gardens, eat what you produce, marry, and have children and help them to grow and find partners in marriage. Seek peace and prosperity for the fallen world to which you have been exiled. Pray for that world because, temporary though it is, if it prospers you also will prosper. And don't despair. I love you and I have not forgotten you. This fallen world, too, will pass.'

My dad, too, often used the words of that well-known adage. I loved my dad dearly, and I miss him greatly. He was my best friend, but dad would be the first to admit that he was not a learned man. I doubt that he ever read Jeremiah. I may be wrong about that, but I am even more certain that he never read Victor Hugo who penned words of encouragement similar to that adage 'This too shall pass', when he wrote in *Les Misérables* 'Even the darkest night will end, and the sun will rise.' Sometimes we need to remind ourselves that the sun will rise tomorrow. But if dad had not read Jeremiah, or Victor Hugo, he certainly knew that adage; 'This too will pass'.

I heard my dad say those words to me many times when he knew that I was hurting. I remember the end of my first teenage romance. For two years Helen had been the love of my life but, alas, Helen decided that I was not the love of her life. I was distraught, beside myself with grief, but my dad put a consoling arm around me and said 'This won't be the last time that this happens to you, son. You're hurting now but you will get over this. This too will pass.' And then, with the glint in his eye that I recognised so well, he said to me 'Let's go fishing.'

Fishing was my dad's panacea for almost all of life's ills. I was born and raised in an inland country town, far from the coast, so our fishing was restricted to inland river fishing and I grew up loving the rivers. We fished in many rivers, all of them were different and some were quite some distance from our home. I can see, in my mind's eye, the rivers from my youth, all of them with their own unique character – shallow water babbling over smooth river stones, rapid running water splashing against the huge rocks which seem to grow out of the river's bed, the rustle of river reeds where slower water makes them sway and dance in perfect unison, the murmur of a gentle breeze which blows through the eucalypts and which causes the overhanging willows to sigh as they gently sweep the surface of the water. But, if all the rivers were different, and they were, then what they had in common was a sense of peace and tranquillity – the capacity to refresh a man's spirit, and to nurture that of a young boy.

In all honesty, we rarely caught many fish but that was less important than spending time together in an environment that we both loved. We'd sit on the riverbank, my dad and I, our fishing lines wound around Coca-Cola bottles, glass ones in those days, for the Coca-Cola bottles had that gentle narrowing of diameter in the middle of them rather like the waistline of a shapely woman – just perfect for winding a fishing line onto, and that is one of the first things that my dad taught me to do.

We'd throw our lines out into the river with a worm or a yabby as bait and we'd then push the neck of the Coca-Cola bottle into the mud. Then, we'd break a twig off a tree, stick it into the mud and wind the line around the top of the twig so that if a fish were silly enough to take our bait, we would see the twig jerk back and forth as the fish pulled at the line. Occasionally we would pull in the line and check that the bait was still there. Occasionally, if it were a hot day, we would strip off and go skinny dipping. Occasionally we would even catch a fish. But most of the time we just talked and soaked up the peace and the beauty of the rivers.

To us, the rivers were God's gallery where He displayed the wonder and the glory of his wonderful and beautiful creation, but they were also my dad's classroom where he passed on to me the things which he held to be important and which would shape me for the rest of my life. The important lessons of life I learned from my dad, most of them on a riverbank somewhere. And perhaps the first lesson that I ever learned on a riverbank, as I sat there with my dad teaching me, was that 'going fishing' has absolutely nothing to do with catching fish, that it has everything to do with refreshing and calming the mind and the heart. And that is an important place to find. Others will find that place in their own way but for us it was found in the company of each other, on the riverbanks. No matter where or how you find it, it is in that place and within that mindset that you can come to a peaceful acceptance of the fact that, whatever the situation in which you find yourself, whatever might be troubling you, this too will pass. And when I look back on it now, I recall that whenever we came home from those idyllic times by the river, mother would never ask 'Did you catch anything?' but rather, 'Did you have a good time?' Dad must have taught her the same things, I guess.

We humans are amazingly complex creatures and sometimes, even, we are contradictions within ourselves. When we find ourselves beset by some form of trial or suffering it is easy to believe that it is going to last indefinitely. We cannot see a way forward, there is no light at the end of the tunnel, and it is sometimes difficult to believe that it is ever going to end. Many people, probably most, can tell of times of suffering in their lives which seemed so intense, so dark, that they thought it unlikely ever to end. But in the main, we are more resilient that we might have thought and in most cases the suffering does end, perhaps gradually, perhaps slowly fading over time, or sometimes with God's grace allowing us to come to the place where we can live with it.

Sometimes, to be sure, deep scarring from painful experiences can remain and can cause us to be vulnerable to, and wary of, being hurt again. Depending upon the nature of the hurt and the suffering which we have experienced, that may turn out, for a season, to be a good thing; a wise and prudent response that allows us time to heal. But in time we should be striving, with God's help, to move on, and when the time is right, we should be ready to let it go – to let it be carried away by the river of life and to let the sun rise on a new day.

But there is a sting in the tail of that adage 'This too shall pass', and it is one which we often neglect. We rightly fall back on the words 'this too shall pass' when we are enduring difficult times and at such times it is a message of hope and encouragement. Most of us, certainly all optimists, would like to believe that the application of the adage ends there, with the promise of better days ahead. After all, that is how we would like it to be, and so we often fail to consider the flipside of those words. That is to say that when things are going well and life is rosy, we tend not to turn our mind to the fact that the adage serves as a reminder that *all* human and material conditions are transient, be they good or bad. In such circumstances the words are a prudent reminder, even a warning that the good times, too, shall pass and the troubles which Jesus promised us will come. It speaks to us of the fact that change is one of the few constants in the human experience of life in this fallen world. It seems almost cyclic. The hard and difficult times will pass and will turn to better times ahead, and the good and happy times, too, will pass and troubles will come. It is part of the cycle of the life that all of us, Christians, and non-Christians alike, must endure as if on a roller-coaster.

King Solomon wrote:

The sun rises and the sun sets, and hurries back to where it rises. The wind blows to the south and turns to the north; round and round it goes, ever returning on its course.... What has been will be again, what has been done will be done again; there is nothing new under the sun. [9]

I doubt that Solomon was referring only to the laws of natural physics which govern this earth, and the universe. I am inclined to believe that he was also reflecting upon the frustration of dark and difficult times recurring in our lives.

On examination, Solomon's words do seem depressing, and even hint at hopelessness and despair. Indeed, Solomon commences the book of Ecclesiastes with very depressing words:

Meaningless! Meaningless, says the Teacher. Utterly meaningless! Everything is meaningless![10]

Now, that's an uplifting and positive opening to a book, don't you think? We could be forgiven for reading those words and just giving up on life. I am reminded that I once had a neighbour who was something of a grump. One of his favourite expressions, and one which distressed me greatly, was 'Life's a bitch, and then you die!' I doubt he's ever read Ecclesiastes but, if he did read it, I am sure that he would point to that first verse and say 'There! See! That's what I'm talking about.' And while most of us, hopefully, do not reach those depths of hopelessness, many have struggled with those eternal questions – What's it all about? What is the use? Why are we here? Is that all there is? What is the purpose? In fact, does life have a purpose at all?

Have you ever been there? Ever asked why we kill ourselves working, just so that we can afford to eat and live, so that we can do it again tomorrow? Ever asked whether what we are doing in this life really makes any difference? Solomon asked the same question:

> *What does man gain from all his labour at which he toils under the sun? Generations come and generations go, but the earth remains forever.*[11]

There is some conjecture about when Solomon wrote Ecclesiastes, but it seems likely that he wrote it toward the end of his life. As a young man, as many of us do at that stage of life, he probably thought that he had all the answers, after all he is renowned as perhaps the wisest man who ever lived. As a young man he was building the temple of God, building his extravagant palace, building his kingdom, and entertaining kings and queens from the far ends of the earth. And yet, toward the end of his life here he is searching for the meaning in life. And we should put this into perspective; Solomon had it all! He had power, wealth, and wisdom such as never had been seen. He had a secure kingdom, profitable foreign trade relations, seven hundred wives and three hundred concubines (though perhaps most of us would consider that something that we could live without). He had it all, but at the end of his life the things he lacked were contentment and sense of purpose. And if Solomon, a mighty king, the wisest man who ever lived with all his wealth and power, questions the meaning of life and whether, in fact, there is any meaning, what chance you and me?

The problem is that Solomon, and my former neighbour, and at times we ourselves, spend too much time navel gazing. We are looking at our life here under the sun and trying to find purpose within ourselves. It is not there. As Solomon recognised, 'there is nothing new under the sun'.[12] Our purpose in life has absolutely nothing to do with ourselves. If you are looking within, and turning to self-help books, you are not going to find it. Our purpose is in a God who created us for *his* purpose. To find our purpose we look towards God's purpose, which is nothing less than the rescuing of his good creation through the renewing of the entire cosmos.

Herein is found the promise of the ultimate passing of all things, the 'expected end'[13] in God's words, the passing of this fallen world. For the promise throughout scripture is that at the end of history God is going to intervene in a wonderful and almost unimaginable way to renew the entire cosmos, and us with it. John writes in the Revelation that he saw '*a new heaven and a new earth for the first heaven and the first earth* [this fallen world] *had passed away*'[14] (words in brackets are those of the author), and he further goes on to talk about the New Jerusalem, the Kingdom of Heaven, coming down to the new earth and the glory of God pouring out of it to fill the entire new earth. The Revelation foretells a time when tears and sorrow, pain, suffering and even death will be no more, '*for the old order of things has passed-away*'[15]. Yes, this tired old fallen world and its troubles are included when we say, 'This too shall pass.'

And in his grace God has given us purpose by preparing for us a role in building for his Kingdom on earth by planting those rose bushes. That is our purpose, not the cyclic rollercoaster ride here and now under the sun. Our purpose has been prepared for each one of us before the foundations of the world. We find our purpose in working towards the coming of God's Kingdom on earth. That is our purpose and our hope.

Things That Shall NOT Pass

'This too shall pass.' What, exactly, does that mean? We have been considering this adage to say that all things shall pass, all positive things and all negative things, all suffering and all joy, all good things and all evil things, everything has its time and will pass away. And, in the main, that is true, but it is not quite true for some things will never pass. God has told us that his love is 'everlasting',[16] from time everlasting to time everlasting. We have God's promise that his love shall never pass. And God's faithfulness, too, shall never pass. His promises are set in stone and sealed with the blood of his Son who will return to rule forever over the Kingdom of Heaven on earth, in which there will be no more death or mourning or crying or pain or suffering, and of which there will be no end.

And what of us? We know that this physical life that we are given to live within this fallen world is fleeting and that it will end. The bodies which we inhabit in the here and now will deteriorate, they will perish and die. Those of us who have placed our trust and our faith in Jesus Christ, however, know that that is not the end. If our temporal life should end before Christ returns then we know that our souls will be cared for and ministered to by the Lord Jesus Christ himself, until the day of his return, the day of resurrection. At that point we will be resurrected to a new physical and spiritual reality with a body which is incorruptible, imperishable, and which will live eternally in the Kingdom with our Lord and our God.

There is, of course, another alternative. Some who have put their faith in Jesus Christ and accepted God's salvation will still be living on that day of Christ's return, and that may well include you and me. If we are among that number then at that point in time our temporal lives will end and we, too, will be transformed in the twinkling of an eye, into that same new physical and spiritual reality, with perfect, imperishable, and eternal bodies. We will then be caught up in the air to meet the returning Christ and the resurrected saints, and then come with them into the Kingdom of Heaven, on earth.

The apostle Paul made this crystal clear when he wrote to the church in Thessalonica:

> *Brothers and sisters, we do not want you to be uninformed about those who sleep in death, so that you do not grieve like the rest of mankind, who have no hope. For we believe that Jesus died and rose again, and so we believe that God will bring with Jesus those who have fallen asleep in him. According to the Lord's word, we tell you that we who are still alive, who are left until the coming of the Lord, will certainly not precede those who have fallen asleep. For the Lord himself will come down from heaven, with a loud command, with the voice of the archangel and with the trumpet call of God, and the dead in Christ will rise first. After that, we who are still*

alive and are left will be caught up together with them in the clouds to meet the Lord in the air. And so, we will be with the Lord forever.[17]

In the meantime, we continue to live in exile but with the promise that this too shall pass. Yes, along the way we will have to deal with those ups and downs of life, with those troubles which Jesus promised we would face in this world. Get used to it, deal with it with the help and comfort of the Holy Spirit, and then get back to your purpose of planting those rose bushes. And as we do so we should remember the words of the apostle Paul writing to the church in Corinth:

Therefore, my dear brothers and sisters, stand firm. Let nothing move you. Always give yourselves fully to the work of the Lord, because you know that your labour in the Lord is not in vain.[18]

Our labour in the Lord is not in vain. It will count for something. It will not be thrown on the scrap heap. It will not pass away. It will be perpetuated. That rose garden is not going to be bulldozed and turned into a parking lot. Those rose bushes will not pass away, they will live forever.

1. 2 Corinthians 4:17-18 (NLT)
2. Jeremiah 31:3-4
3. Isaiah 39:6 & 2 Kings 20:17
4. John 16:33
5. Jeremiah 29:1-23
6. Jeremiah 29:4-7
7. Jeremiah 29:11
8. Ibid. (KJV)
9. Ecclesiastes 1:5-6 & 9
10. Ecclesiastes 1:2
11. Ecclesiastes 1:3-4
12. Ecclesiastes 1:9
13. Jeremiah 29:11 (KJV)
14. Revelation 21:1
15. Revelation 21:4
16. Jeremiah 31:3
17. 1 Thessalonians 4:13-17
18. 1 Corinthians 15:58

Chapter 4
Don't Beat Up on Yourself

As I write these words the holy season of Easter is drawing near. I mention that because I am reminded that a few years back I was given a gift at this time, something which turned out to be a wonderful gift. A dear friend bought me a series of daily devotions delivered online during the period of Lent. Maybe she thought I needed to ramp up my devotion time somewhat. She was probably right. Each day a new devotional guide turned up in my email inbox, and it continued until Easter Sunday.

Now, I have to say that Lent had never been very prominent on my agenda. I had never really disciplined myself to the practice of self-denial during Lent. I did teach for many years in an Anglican Church School where the practice of self-denial during Lent was encouraged amongst the students and staff, but when asked 'What are you giving up for Lent this year, Ian?' I would usually give some flippant response like 'I think maybe this year I'll give up lettuce. Yeah, that should do. I'll give up lettuce. Maybe brussels sprouts too.'

But the devotionals which I had been given seemed to take a different approach. The writer of those devotions suggested that the long-established custom of giving up treats, chocolates, caffeinated or sugary beverages, alcohol, or tobacco (or even lettuce) is just surface stuff; that choosing to give up something good for something a bit less good is a play-it-safe strategy. And I think that is right. I doubt that Lent is about a temporary abstinence from over-indulgence. If Lent is about anything, it is about coming closer to God through renewal and transformation, for whilst we, as Christians, might have been converted once in a flash of forgiveness and grace, I believe that we are transformed constantly, gradually, little by little, with a drip-system-grace.

Sometimes, however, we move away of the dripline; we drift away, putting space between ourselves and God. Lent can be a chance for a fresh start, for a deliberate return to the grace dripline. So, since receiving that gift of on-line devotions at the time of Lent a few years back, I have given up the same thing each year. I give up something that is precious to me – I give up time. Giving up time means finding more time to be with God, it is a deliberate return to God. Of course, I know that we need not wait for Lent to roll around each year to draw closer to God. It should be the main objective of our lives, daily, to examine our lives and our spiritual journey, in order to ensure that we are still walking with the Lord, and I do try to do that. But the approach of the holy season of Easter is a special time, a time of serious contemplation, and that includes introspectively contemplating our own lives and how we are traveling in respect to God.

How are you traveling right now? Sometimes an accurate answer to that question eludes us. That is where Christian friendship is so important. The fact is, we are often hard on ourselves. It is easy to be your own harshest critic. We take note of all the ways we fall short, and that is important, but we fail to notice the ways we have been pleasing to God. Christian friends who love us with a godly love can give us a more balanced picture. Real friends will tell us honestly where we have fallen short. But they will also tell us not to beat up on ourselves. And they will remind us of our good deeds and good dispositions. Spiritual friends will help us to live for God daily, hourly. I am grateful that I have such friends, and I am particularly grateful that I have that one friend who sent me that lovely gift of devotions delivered on-line during Lent. Thank you, my friend. You know who you are!

I don't know about you, but I sometimes, too often, find myself making the same stupid mistakes over, and over again. Not all those mistakes are sins, of course. Some are, but some are just mistakes as I go about my normal life and my work. An example: numerous times I have parked the car in the garage and left it there with the lights turned on. Of course, I come out next morning, jump in the car, and find that I have a drained battery. It is not the end of the world, most people have probably done that, and with some help from the neighbour I can usually get the car started. But, in the meantime, I'll let myself know all about it; 'You idiot! You've done it again!'

Now, issues like that are mere irritants, usually with no real and lasting consequence. I can berate myself for making that same mistake yet again, promise myself that it will never happen again, knowing all the time that it probably will, and move on. After all, nobody is perfect, and failure is part of the human experience.

But some of those silly mistakes that I make over and over again are more than that; some of them are sins, and just like the small mistake of leaving the car lights on, I find myself committing those sins again and again. Why don't I learn not to do those things? I think that there are probably three reasons which work in combination to lead me into those sins. Firstly, like most of us, I am a creature of habit. It is easy to fall back on past practices. Secondly, Satan knows my weaknesses. For example, he knows that there is not much point in tempting me to shoplift because I am not going to do that. But he does also know the matters in which I am vulnerable; he knows which buttons to press. And thirdly, Satan knows just when to press those buttons. And, invariably, Satan pushes those buttons at a time when I have neglected my relationship with God. Those are the times when I have moved away from the grace dripline and my spiritual battery has been drained. Spiritually, I am at a low point; I am vulnerable, and Satan knows that there is no better time to push my buttons.

It goes without saying, of course, that the way to avoid this is always to remain close to God. But sometimes we drift away. We are weak, we are forgetful, and sometimes inattentive human beings, and too often we wander towards our own agenda and away from God's agenda. I have a facility in my car called 'Lane Drift Alert' (LDA) and if I allow the car to drift across the line dividing the traffic lanes then I hear a series of short beeps which is effectively saying to me 'Wake up! Get back in your lane!' I could turn it off, but I leave it on because I am quite surprised just how often I allow the car to drift across that line. It is interesting, and I thank God for the fact, that I do have that same facility in my life to remind me, 'You have wandered! Get back to being close to God!' It is called the Holy Spirit, but for forgetful and inattentive human beings the nudging of the Holy Spirit can be easy to ignore; almost as if I had the LDA beeps turned off. And it is when we continue to ignore the nudging of the Spirit that we find ourselves in the wrong lane and away from that dripline of grace. We know that, just as we know that it is stupid to leave the car lights on, but still we do it. All too often we simply allow ourselves to drift away from God and away from his agenda for us, and Satan smiles.

What, then, is God's agenda for us? Well, God's agenda for us operates on two levels – two levels which combine to cover every moment of our lives. God does have what we might call a 'whole-of-life agenda' for us, a great plan which is nothing less than God's purpose for our lives; the reason we were put here on this earth. Knowing that purpose, which is revealed to us by the Holy Spirit, and with God's help living out that purpose, is to fulfill God's perfect plan for our lives, a plan that God worked out especially for me and for you, before creation. That is God's 'whole-of-life agenda' for us, our course in life, and it includes our career, our marriage partner, our family relationships, and the missional roles that we are led into by the Holy Spirit. Our lives are never truly fulfilling unless we are living within that agenda.

But God also has for us a continuous, round-the-clock, agenda. He has great plans for us minute-by-minute, and whilst we must seek out God's purpose for our lives, our 'whole-of-life agenda', so too we should be asking, 'What is God's agenda for me this morning when I leave home and commute to the office, what is his agenda for me as I mix and interact with my work colleagues, what is his agenda for me this evening when I share the evening meal with my family and share quality time with my children?' I cannot tell you what God's 'whole-of-life agenda' is for you. That is something that you must work out with God – it took me long enough to work out my own purpose. But I can tell you that God's 'minute-by-minute agenda' for you is quite simply that you should know his joy. Isn't that great? God is saying to us 'I have plans for you today, my son, my daughter. I have plans for your day at the office, I have plans for the time you will spend commuting and plans for the time that you will spend chatting with work colleagues over lunch and plans for the time you will spend with your family tonight. And they are great plans – live today in my joy.'

At the Passover feast that we remember as 'The Last Supper' Jesus was preparing the disciples for the fact that he would soon be taken from them. He knew the confusion and the despair that they were going to face within a few hours, and he comforted them with wonderful promises. He promised to send The Comforter, The Holy Spirit, to guide them, to comfort them, to encourage them, to embolden them, to pour out God's love upon their lives. What an awesome promise that was and is. And he promised them something else, something that is immeasurable, he promised his joy.

'I have told you this', said Jesus, *'so that my joy may be in you and that your joy may be complete.'*[1]

So, what is this joy that Jesus gives us, often called 'The Joy of the Lord'? Is it a feeling of assurance and belonging within the soul? Yes, it is. Is it the knowledge that we are greatly loved? Yes, it is. Is it the confidence that God is in control of every aspect of our lives, and that God is working to renew his good creation, including mankind? Yes, it is certainly that! Is it the assurance that no matter what the future holds for us as individuals, no matter how many of those deep troughs we must pass through along the way, God is in control and therefore everything is going to be all right in the end? Yes, it is that too.

Is it a feeling of contentment and happiness? Well, yes, it can be that, but we should not confuse happiness with joy. Happy times are wonderful, and we thank God for those times, and we hope that those happy times will continue. But happiness is not the joy of the Lord. We know that Jesus promised that we will have trouble in this world, that we will face difficult times, unhappy times, and when those times come, happiness can be fleeting and fickle. Happiness is dictated by circumstances; we all know that. But the joy of the Lord endures, regardless of circumstances. Happiness can ebb and flow and can be derived from many sources. Even Satan can bring you happiness, for a season – Satan will never bring you joy, for he himself is incapable of real joy. That is why he comes constantly knocking at our door, wanting to steal our joy.

The online encyclopedia of Biblical Christianity defines the joy of the Lord, thus:

> Joy is a state of mind and an orientation of the heart. It is a settled state of contentment, confidence, and hope.[2]

Furthermore, let us remember, the joy that Jesus gives us is *his* joy. Do you see what that means? It is *his* state of mind, it is *his* orientation of the heart, it is *his* contentment, *his* confidence, and *his* hope. No wonder Satan wants to steal it!

Why would you choose to live any other way? But it is something that we do have to choose, day by day, minute by minute. Too easily, and too often, we allow our days to get off to a bad start – perhaps being distracted and unresponsive to the kids at the breakfast table, perhaps just a grunted response or maybe even just a surly nod when a colleague greets us at the office, perhaps just the body language that says to everyone 'leave me alone!' What has happened here is that the great joy-stealer, Satan, has found an opening, just a crack, and he has come in like a thief in the night and taken away that joy. Perhaps we have just allowed ourselves to drift away from that dripline of grace – it could be because of some sin and the accompanying feeling of guilt. And that is all it takes. Satan does not need us to push the door off its hinges – a little opening, a small crack, will do. And I know that when that happens to me my response is the same as when I leave the car lights burning; 'You idiot! You've done it again! You've let yourself down! You've let God down!' At times like that I feel that I am a failure. I get down on myself, I just do not want to be around other people, and I feel that God is getting ready to unload a truckload of wrath on me. Fortunately, God is far more patient with us than we sometimes are with ourselves. The psalmist tells us:

For he knows how weak we are; he remembers we are only dust.[3]

Praise God for that! Without that we would all spend much of our time wandering around like lost dogs.

Incidentally, I used to have a dog, now long gone to doggy-heaven. She was a lovely dog, a happy dog, always running around and enjoying herself (and digging bottomless holes in my garden). And, although she knew that I might get angry with her from time to time, she knew that she would never be beaten. I would say she had a fortunate and an enjoyable life. I would even say that she had a lot of joy in her life; she knew contentment living in and destroying my garden, she had confidence that the food bowl would be refilled every day. But, as you may have gathered from her destructive work in the garden, she also had a mischievous streak. I sometimes threatened to take her back to the dog shelter from where I had rescued her. I never would have done so, of course, but there were times when she tested me.

Her name was Patch. Yes, I know that Patch sounds a bit masculine but, you see, she was mostly white with a large black patch over one eye. Logic said there was no other name for her. I did think about calling her Nelson, or perhaps Horatio, but of course those are also masculine names and so would have resulted in the same problem, so she got stuck with Patch. Truthfully, I don't think that it mattered because I am sure that she thought her name was 'No, No, Bad Dog!' Anyone who has owned a dog will have an endless list of their dog's indiscretions and misdemeanours but let me tell you of just a few things that Patch got up to.

Bleary eyed, I wandered out onto the back deck for my morning coffee to find one of the large ceramic pots on its side, broken to pieces, and the plant and soil spilled onto the deck. 'That's strange,' I thought, 'I didn't think the easterly wind was that strong last night.' Then it occurred to me that there is another possibility. I looked around, but it was too late. Patch was headed for the doghouse with her tail between her legs, a sure sign of guilt.

Then there was the cordless telephone which disappeared from the table on the deck, and is still missing, no doubt buried in the back yard somewhere. I tried to call it, but I could not hear it ringing and, yes, I checked the doghouse – she was not making phone calls. I spoke to Patch firmly about the phone, showed her another identical phone hoping that she would then lead me to the missing phone, but her only response was to slink away to the doghouse.

On yet another day I found a bedsheet torn from the clothesline and dragged around the yard. This one got the better of me and I decided to yell at her. It was too late – she had already taken refuge in the doghouse. I yelled anyway.

The strange thing is that after every such incident Patch knew that I was angry but, also after every incident, ten minutes later she'd be back, rubbing against me, nudging me, licking my leg, wanting to be patted. It would have served no purpose for me to have yelled at her again because she'd already forgotten; 'What bedsheet? What phone?' She'd moved on. Dogs, I have decided, live in the present, in the here-and-now. Patch would put things behind her very quickly and move on. It is not a bad way to be. We could learn a lot from Patch and the way that she would let go of the past. I am working on that and I'll get there. It would probably be easier if I were a dog.

How do we maintain the necessary balance? How do we reach that place where we can acknowledge our shortcomings, and confess them, all whilst continually living the joy that Jesus gives us? It is, I believe, an attitudinal acceptance that Jesus wants us to live in that joy and not to dwell upon the past; not to continually return to our failures as a dog might return to its vomit. We know that Jesus told us that in this world we will have troubles, we know that sometimes those troubles are huge, we know that we are weak, that in the words of the psalmist 'we are only dust'[4] and we know that all too often we fail; we fail ourselves and we fail God. Those things are trial enough within themselves and as we seek to deal with those trials, we certainly do not need to add to our troubles by blaming ourselves or getting down on ourselves.

Beating up on ourselves is a tactic that Satan uses to steal our joy. We must not allow him to do that to us. That is not to say that we should not recognise failures but rather that we do not allow those failures to hold us down in guilt and shame. Acknowledge our failures before God, ask for his forgiveness, ask for the guidance of the Holy Spirit to help us to avoid those failures again, accept God's grace, and then move on together with him. Get back quickly into the dripline of grace and live in the joy that Jesus gives us.

Forgiving myself and moving on is something that I sometimes struggle with. God has forgiven me, I know that, but still, I sometimes find myself dwelling on stupid and sinful things in my past. It is not guilt, for as I said I know that God has forgiven me. No, it is not guilt; it's shame. God's forgiveness is instantaneous the moment we turn back to God and confess our sins in genuine repentance. Getting over the shame, on the other hand, sometimes takes much longer because it means forgiving ourselves. It should not take longer – but for me it does. Some people, including me at times, live shackled to their past, they know that they are forgiven but they do not always live in the joy of that forgiveness.

Other people, and I sometimes fall into this group as well, hold onto the past because of the fond memories that it holds for them; 'Do you remember when we used to ……? Wasn't that great?'

Remembering good and happy times is perfectly fine. At 70+ years of age I still attend an annual reunion of a church youth group and catch up with friends from my teen years. It is fun, and we laugh a lot when remembering some of the things we got up to. There is nothing wrong with enjoying the company of your friends and reminiscing about the past with them, but we should always be looking forward to the joys and triumphs that God has in store for us, yet to come. Dwelling on the past is a pointless exercise; recognise it yes, enjoy it yes, but decide not to dwell on it. We surely cannot change the past, nor can we bring it back.

As for the future, as Christians our future inheritance in glory is assured but just what tomorrow holds for us here on this earth is anyone's guess. While we are here on this earth all we have is today. So, I encourage you to live your life in God's joy today. If you need to be comforted in sorrow, then seek comfort. If you need to mourn then mourn. If you need to praise your children or your spouse or your neighbours, then praise them. If you need to celebrate how great things were in the past, then celebrate. If you need to forgive your spouse or your neighbour then forgive, if you need to be forgiven then ask forgiveness. If you need to put things right with God and ask His forgiveness, then do so. But then move on, for God has not given us a spirit of fear, but of power and of love and of a sound mind.[5]

1. John 15:11
2. https://www.theopedia.com/joy
3. Psalm 103:14 (NLT)
4. Ibid.
5. 2 Timothy 1:7

Chapter 5
Be Kind to Yourself

This an important chapter, indeed it is a critical chapter and yet as I begin to write this chapter I do so with a sense of trepidation. This will be a relatively short chapter because, in fact, it deals with an issue about which I know little – managing mental health.

I confess up front that I am not an expert on mental health or on how to manage a mental illness. I have no qualifications and no professional training as a mental health advisor or facilitator. I *have* had opportunity to observe friends and family members who have suffered various forms of mental illness. As mentioned earlier, I watched my much-loved sister spiral into a form of mental illness which culminated in her tragic death. I was deeply traumatised by that experience and I still carry a huge load of guilt because I was incapable of helping her at the time when she needed me most. And I think that the reason that I was unable to help her was that my own mental health was also being impacted by the situation that we found ourselves in at that time.

I have also been able to observe another dear friend who for many years struggled with deep clinical depression and an anxiety disorder, and who even now needs to manage it carefully. Though I did little more than offer a friendly and compassionate ear from time to time, I am honoured that she trusted me enough to allow me into her pain, and that in some small way I have been able to walk part of that journey with her. Indeed, to a large extent, our friendship grew out of those times of sharing. We now live a great distance apart, but we remain in contact and I look forward to seeing her, and her family, whenever I can.

One thing that I have learned about mental illness is that people who are suffering from a mental illness need one thing above all others – they need hope. Hope that what they are experiencing and what they are living with will pass. Hope that there is a brighter future awaiting them. Hope that there are those who understand them. Hope that there are those who love them and who care about them. My sister died because she believed her future was hopeless, and that is partly my fault. I was unable to give her the hope that she needed. And I believe that, though specialist mental health practitioners and counsellors can be incredibly important, one does not need specialist training or formal qualifications to be a source of hope to those suffering depression or anxiety disorders. Love, gentleness, empathy, care, support, and listening non-judgmentally can go a long way towards giving the hope that people so desperately need.

When I started to write this book, I gave it the title *Glass Half Full* because I wanted it to be a book of hope and encouragement to all who would read it. At that stage I did not realise that I would need to write about mental health. But it is now clear to me that if this book is to be all about hope and encouragement, then this is an issue that I need to explore here. Though it is likely to be short, and will certainly be inexpertly written, it may be the most important chapter in the book.

Important

If you are a person who has no mental health issues, then please do not think that you can skip this chapter and move on to the next. I say that because:

* At any one time, around 20% of Australians are suffering from mental health issues. That is one in five! There is no reason to assume that you will not become part of that 20% just because everything seems fine right now. You might develop a mental illness.
* At some stage in your life, you will certainly be able to give hope to someone who is suffering from a mental illness. I pray that in these pages you will be able to learn some strategies for helping in that way.

So, what I am intending to do here is to offer some strategies for coping with a mental illness, for notwithstanding the fact that I have little experience or qualifications in the field of mental health, I do have one thing; I care. That is a simple and yet a crucial starting point; I care. I care about those who are struggling with a mental illness, and I care about those who don't have a mental illness but who are struggling to walk part of that journey with a friend or a loved one who does. And caring is the starting point; by all means, add professional skills if that is your calling, but it starts with a caring heart. It is my hope and my prayer that both those who are directly suffering from a mental illness, and those who are struggling to care for them, will find some helpful strategies here; that they will gain some measure of hope.

I want to be able to suggest a few strategies for two groups of people, and for all of us:

> 1. For the trusted friend, the one who comes alongside to help walk the journey.
> 2. For the person who is experiencing the very real effects of a mental illness of any kind.

1. For the Trusted Friend
* Consider it an honour that your friend has allowed you into his/her pain. It shows that you have the attributes of a true friend. Try to let that honour that you feel show through in all your dealings with the person that you are helping.
* Tread carefully. Be gentle. You are helping a person whose emotional state may be very fragile.
* If you know a person who you suspect *might* be struggling with a mental illness then come alongside that person as a friend, let the friendship develop closer, and earn that person's trust. Don't wait to be invited, but don't be pushy either. Acting with discernment, it is okay to ask about the person's mental health state. It shows the person that you are not afraid to talk about that topic, that it isn't a taboo topic with you, and it normalises the

experience. You can venture there and, if the person doesn't want to discuss it, he or she will let you know.
* Find the right place to talk. Outside in the sunshine of a beautiful day is likely to be better than a dark and gloomy room. Being outside, perhaps in a garden or on a veranda/deck also gives you the opportunity to talk about how beautiful the world is.
* Listen a lot and talk little. The person you are there to help will probably be self-absorbed or self-focused. Unless you are directly asked, he or she probably does not want to know what is going on in your life, and certainly doesn't want to know your troubles.
* Be compassionate. Remember that 'compassion' means to 'suffer with' (see p.25). If you are inclined to say to the person suffering mental illness "Come on! Snap out of it!" then you do not understand mental health, you are not being compassionate, and you are not the right person. Get out of the way and allow someone more appropriate to step in.
* Most importantly, honour the confidentiality of the relationship. It is not your place to talk to others about the person you are helping. The exception to that would be, of course, if you have reason to believe that the person is likely to harm himself/herself, or others.

2. For the Person Experiencing a Mental Illness

Talk about it

This is certainly easier said than done but confiding in somebody about what you are feeling can do you a power of good. I believe that, difficult though it may be, those who are suffering a mental illness do need someone to talk to, to share what they are experiencing. The first step before that can even happen, of course, is recognising and acknowledging that you do have a mental health problem, and that can be an exceedingly difficult and confronting step. Many people can feel ashamed or embarrassed about their feelings. Many feel that there is some stigma associated with mental health. That may have been the case in generations past but thankfully, in today's world, we are more enlightened and recognise mental illness for what it is – a medical condition from which anyone can suffer. Many sufferers, however, still worry about what others will think of them and are very reluctant to open-up about it with another person. Sadly, if that persists then it is likely that the person will not receive the help and the treatment that they need. So, my friend, if you are experiencing depression, anxiety, obsessive compulsive disorder, eating disorders, or any other form of mental illness, I encourage you, I most strongly encourage you, to seek out a trusted friend, someone who you know can be relied upon to come alongside you with compassion, to listen to you, and to walk the journey with you. A problem shared might not be a problem solved, but it is a big step in the right direction.

Seek professional help

Some people who are enduring a mental illness will shy away from seeking professional help. It stems from the issue that we have already seen; that they can feel ashamed or embarrassed about sharing their feelings. It is thus understandable that some sufferers of mental illness will think that they will be thought of as being weak because they need to turn to others for professional help. If you are suffering from a mental illness, then I really implore you not to think like that. To acknowledge that you need help and support in difficult times is a sign of great personal strength. It is certainly not a weakness; just the opposite in fact, because it takes courage to reach out for professional help. If you are suffering from a mental illness, and you do not know where you should turn to for that professional help, start with your GP. Talk to your GP about your situation; about what you are experiencing, and your GP will certainly be able to arrange for you to get the help that you need. It is important, also, to seek that help as early as possible. Do not think that you will be able to just 'tough it out'; an early intervention is the key to a shorter and easier recovery.

Take Good Care of Yourself

I understand that taking on suggestions which are intended to help you feel better, and making those strategies part of your routine, can be a daunting prospect. Remember that different things will work for different people. So, do not be put off by the list of suggestions below; if one does not work for you move onto another. But when you try one of these strategies, I encourage you to give it a fair trial. It might not seem to be making much difference in the short term, but you may find that over the course of a few weeks you are feeling better. It is my hope and my prayer that you will find at least some of these strategies to be helpful.

Me Time

* Set aside some ME time for yourself. Every day set aside some time to do things that you enjoy doing. Even better, *plan* your me time. For example, plan that *tomorrow I am going to spend an hour writing my journal,* or *playing the piano,* or *writing a short story,* or *working on a painting,* or *meeting with a friend for coffee.* By planning your me time, not only do you find yourself doing an enjoyable activity, but because it is pre-planned you may also experience joy in the anticipation of doing it.
* It is a good idea if some of your 'me time activities' are longer term projects; something that you can come back to again and again. That helps to keep you future focused. Again, you may find joy in the anticipation of getting back to it, and there is a rewarding sense of achievement when the project is completed.
* Creative activities can be a great help. That is why I have suggested writing stories, painting, playing a musical instrument, etc.

Enjoy the Great Outdoors

Interacting with nature can reduce stress and anxiety and lift your spirits. Take the dog for a walk. Dogs are wonderful therapy; they don't know how to do anything other than return your love and affection. Explore local parks and public gardens taking time to appreciate the birds, the flowers, and the trees. Better still, do it with a friend. If you happen to live near the ocean, take a walk along the beach; get your feet wet and feel the sand between your toes. Sunshine helps regulate your mood and relieve stress and anxiety, so even sitting in the sunshine on your back deck can help.

Develop a Healthy Lifestyle
* Be kind to yourself and to your physical body. Develop a healthy sleep routine and eat well with plenty of fruit and vegetables.
* Keep active and get plenty of exercise. Exercise is particularly important for mental health, for two reasons: firstly, exercise burns off the extra adrenaline that is pumping though our bodies when we experience anxiety, and secondly, it releases feel-good chemicals, the endorphins. So, develop a regular (at least daily) exercise regime.
* Take pride in your appearance by making sure you are well groomed and well dressed. All these things help you to feel better about yourself and improve your sense of wellbeing.

Accept Yourself for What You Are

Stop trying to be perfect. Nobody is perfect, so if you try to be perfect you are setting yourself up for failure. You are like everyone else; we have strengths, and we have weaknesses. Sometimes we get it right, and sometimes we fail. Sometimes we achieve our goals, sometimes we fall short. That is life, for all of us, and you are no different. All that any of us can do, is to be ourselves and accept ourselves for what we are. And you are nothing less than God's good creation made in his own image. Remember that.

Respect Yourself

You are a worthy individual; created by God in his own image. We should all have respect for God and for his good creation of which we are a part. Having self-respect means having confidence in yourself, in your thoughts, your opinions, your decisions and your actions. It means living with grace, honour, and dignity. It means trusting yourself, making your own decisions and not allowing others to dictate your value.

Forgive Yourself

We all mess up from time to time. Remember, none of us is perfect. Maybe you failed to stand up and assert yourself, maybe you allowed someone to walk all over you. Maybe you were not brave enough to take an opportunity. It happens. It happens to all of us. Remember that you are a worthy individual, show yourself kindness, stop blaming yourself, forgive yourself whilst resolving to learn from that experience.

Remind Yourself that "What I Am is Enough".

We've all had times in our lives when we have thought that we don't measure up; *I'm not beautiful/handsome enough,* or *I'm not clever enough,* or *I don't live up to other people's expectations.* What we must do at those times is to remind ourselves that we are God's good creation – I am enough just as I am, I am worthy, I am meant to live my life with joy.

Treat Yourself Now and Then

There is no need to max out the credit card, but if there is something that you would like, something that would make you happy, then go buy it. Buy it as a gift for yourself and ask the store to gift wrap it. It is a gift – for you. You deserve it!

Things Outside Our Control

Sometimes events in the world can weigh heavily on our thoughts and impact on our mental health. At the time of writing the entire world is struggling with the seemingly unstoppable spread of the deadly Covid-19 Coronavirus Pandemic. A great deal will be said about this situation in a later chapter, but we do need to recognise, here, that the mental health of many people is being adversely affected by this pandemic and by the ways in which it has changed our lives. I am aware that my own mental health is being tested and impacted upon during this time, because being isolated at home can be inherently depressing, especially for those who live alone, as I do. What we need to be telling ourselves is that, largely, this event is beyond our control as individuals. We should be praying for the world, for our front-line medical practitioners, and for those searching for a vaccine. Yes, of course, we must take sensible health precautions that otherwise would not be necessary (masks, social distancing, etc.), but let us also remember that life is beautiful, that this is a beautiful world, and that it can be again; let us remind ourselves, and each other, that this too will pass.

Other wider issues can also press upon our consciousness. Perhaps you may find that it is politics that oppress your thoughts, perhaps family issues, perhaps the state of your nation, perhaps global environmental issues, or perhaps the economic uncertainty that is one of the consequences of the pandemic. Sometimes we can feel that the fabric of our society is being rent asunder. I have wonderful American friends who, for the past four years, have felt oppressed and greatly distressed by the unpredictable, irresponsible, and ego-centric actions of their President (Trump). And, though I am not American, I fully understand that. I understand their distress over the racial violence that has divided their country, the anguish that they feel when they see the social unrest in their city streets, and their deep-seated and fully understandable concerns about the political and social divides which seem to have been facilitated, even encouraged, by President Trump. To them, it seemed that their much-loved country was being torn apart, and though they now rejoice in Trump's defeat in the 2020 election they know that it is going to be a long crawl back from the damage that has been done by the Trump legacy. Such issues have the capacity to impact on the mental health of all of us. In my country too, in Australia, many people experience despair and anxiety about the future of our country, and of our people.

So, what can we do when we are confronted with depressing and troublesome issues which are beyond our control? What we must do is to come together and turn to those who love us. We must seek joy and compassion in our relationships by comforting one another, loving one another, and caring for one another. We need to know, and to reassure one another, that we will get through these difficulties. And when we do that, we learn that we are stronger when we stand together, joined by bonds of common affection and care. I am reminded of a story book from my childhood, *The Jungle Book* by Rudyard Kipling. Most of the characters in the stories are jungle animals, but the principal character is a young boy who is raised in the jungle by wolves. There was an important lesson that the wolves taught the boy and, whilst I'm not sure that I remember the precise words of the quote, I know that it was something along the lines of *'The strength of the Pack is in the Wolf, and the strength of the Wolf is in the Pack'*. By coming together, we draw strength from the pack, and we contribute strength to the pack. And that is why I believe that we are stronger when we stand together. A person, no matter how weak, is made strong by the love that he or she gives and by the love that he/she receives.

A Final Word to Those Who Are Struggling with A Mental Illness

And so, my friend, as we come to the end of this chapter, may I just remind you to reach out and to ask for help from others who are more qualified than I. And please know that there are people who love you and care for you. I care for you – I care for you immensely even though I do not know you.

May I also mention that as you share your feelings with that special friend who you trust to walk this journey with you, it is possible that friend may say to you "I will pray for you" or "May I pray with you?" I know that if you are a Christian that you will welcome that offer of prayer. But perhaps you are not a Christian and if that is the case then I urge you to just accept those prayers as a gift of love. Immerse yourself in those prayers and feel the power and the warmth of God's love washing over you.

May you find peace in prayer, and please be kind to yourself.

Chapter 6
The Sum Total of Many Small Victories

The Merriam-Webster dictionary defines perseverance as follows:

continued effort to do or achieve something despite difficulties, failure, or opposition: the action or condition or an instance of persevering

Thus, perseverance is an on-going process until the goal is achieved. It is not a one-off victory of the will that leads to success, rather it leads to success through many small victories.

There is an adage that appears to have been in circulation since at least the time of the Second World War – an expression that is often wrongly attributed to Winston Churchill. It seems impossible to trace the real origins of the expression so I must resort to attributing it to some anonymous individual: 'If you are going through hell, just keep going.' It's an adage that says to us 'Don't stop! Don't give up and set up camp here! Don't dwell on your troubles. Keep moving forward!' It is a message of perseverance in the face of troubles, be they large or small troubles. Sometimes life is just about pure perseverance, about putting one footstep in front of the other. There are times when there is not a lot more that you can do.

Jesus spoke to his disciples, telling them the parable of *The Persistent Widow* who time and time again kept bringing her petition before a judge who was disinclined to give her the justice that she sought and deserved. But the widow never gave up. She kept coming back to the judge to seek justice, until finally she wore him down and he gave her the justice that she sought, if for no other reason than that he just wanted to be rid of her.[1] Jesus was, of course, making the point to his disciples that they should always persevere in faith and in prayer, and never grow faint or give up. In the parable that we know as the parable of *The Persistent Friend*,[2]

Jesus used a different parable scenario to make the same point. For the Christian, that attitude of determined perseverance is underwritten by some of the wonderful promises of our Lord Jesus; none more so than *'Take heart. I have overcome the world.'*[3]

And there are times when just getting through the frustrations and adversities of life in general call for dogged perseverance, whether it is in times of genuine heartache or whether it be just the minor frustration of life's general ups and downs. Paul, in writing his second letter to the church in Corinth speaks of something which he had to endure – he called it 'a thorn in my flesh.'[4] We don't know what it was, but three times, Paul said, he asked God to remove it, but God said 'No'. God's response to Paul was *'My grace is sufficient for you, for my power is made perfect in weakness'.*[5] Acquiring a disciplined habit of perseverance, combined with God's grace, will carry us through most of life's trials.

I used to live in Perth, I think I have mentioned that. I have very good friends in Perth, almost life-long friends who had a beautiful property in the foothills of the Darling Range; a large property with a swimming pool, a tennis court, and the most magnificent trees; all kinds of statuesque palm trees, large frangipani trees, classical and exotic trees from different parts of the world, and the largest pecan nut tree that you will ever see. Local authorities estimated that the pecan tree was more than 100 years old and categorised it as a 'heritage listed asset', meaning that it could not be removed without local government approval. It was, and is, a huge and beautiful tree with a height of about 40 - 45 metres and a spread of about 20 – 25 metres. When I heard that my friends were intending to sub-divide their property and sell half of it, I decided immediately that I would buy that block of land and build my new home on it. The knowledge that I would be able to put a gate in the dividing fence and use the neighbour's pool certainly appealed to me but, in truth, it was the magnificent trees which, more than anything else, attracted me to the property. I just loved those trees, and I was delighted when I found that, after the sub-division, the pecan tree would be within my property. It would be close to the boundary line and almost half of it would overhang the dividing fence between my property and that of my friends, but it would become my tree. My new home was built, and the pecan tree beautifully framed the home and the driveway. I loved living there close to my friends and surrounded by those magnificent trees but, oh my goodness, that pecan tree would cause a lot of work.

It started in spring each year when the tree was almost covered in catkins, thousands upon thousands of long tassel type flowers that wind-pollinate the female flowers thus producing nuts. The catkins are around 15 to 20 centimetres long and each catkin can produce as many as 2.5 million grains of pollen. That is a lot of overkill because only a single grain of pollen is required to pollenate each female flower and produce one pecan nut. Having done their job, the catkins then drop; that is to say, they dropped onto my lawn, onto my deck, onto my driveway, and they filled the storm water guttering on the roof of my house. The catkins turn into small yellow larvae that crawl on the veranda, on the deck and on the driveway, and are then walked into the house. They are truly nasty little things (other than to a female pecan flower), and spring was the season of raking up the catkins.

Summer would see the setting of the nuts on the tree, thousands of them, and the arrival of large flocks of parrots. Pecan nuts have a fibrous covering. Inside that is a harder shell, and inside the harder shell is the edible kernel of the nut. The smaller parrots could break open the fibrous covering, but they were unable to break through the harder shell, though they seem not to accept that as a given fact. They would give up on one nut, drop it, and try another – an act of perseverance without success. They would just keep on trying, without success, to find a nut that they might be able break open. That they never learned says a lot about the limited intelligence of those small parrots. Then there were the large flocks of huge black cockatoos. They could break the nuts. They would arrive in flocks of up to a hundred birds then they'd sit up there all day, breaking off small branches, eating all the nuts on it, then dropping the branch and breaking off another branch – truly destructive birds. Clearing up all the small branches dropped by the cockatoos was a constant task during that season. The tree was so huge that there was no way that I could get up there to pick the nuts, so each year I got only those nuts dropped by the small parrots.

Finally, with my ridiculously small harvest of pecan nuts tucked away, autumn would arrive, and the tree would start to shed all its leaves – thousands upon thousands of them. They filled the storm water roof gutters of my house, they covered the front veranda, they blew under the front door, and they covered the lawn so thickly that the lawn would have died had I not raked them up. They covered the driveway and then the car tyres picked them up and carried them into the garage. Added to that was the embarrassment of seeing my neighbour scowl as he watched my leaves float across the fence line and into his roof gutters (he seemed to forget that it used to be his tree and that for him it has always been thus!) So, I would ignore him and get on with trying to rake up all the leaves, put them in the wheelbarrow and move them around the back of the house where I would spread them on the garden because the back garden was quite sandy and the leaves would break down to form good mulch. But I could not keep up with the leaves – more leaves were falling than I could move.

On a Saturday evening my front lawn would look rather good. On Sunday morning it would look like I had never touched a rake in my life! And so I spent much of my time, and certainly all my weekends, scooping up leaves. At times it was an overwhelming task. To exacerbate the problem, those who have lived in the Perth hills will know that in the foothills the residents have to endure long and persistent periods of strong easterly winds. One year the easterly wind blew over the fence between my house and that of my neighbour. That wind was just something that we had to live with.

There were times when, as I raked the leaves, I thought about how overwhelming life can feel at times. Just as I seemed never to be able to catch up with the falling leaves so too were the challenges of my daily life. Sometimes my life felt like I had never touched a rake and, though I no longer live there with that tree, there are still times when I know that I need to work on getting my life and my habits under control. There are so many things that I struggle to get right – diet (a four-letter word if ever there was one!), exercise, finances, relationships, home maintenance, my personal spiritual growth, my prayer time. Trying to get all those things under control is a bit like raking leaves when the easterly wind is blowing.

How about you? Do you manage those things better than I do or does it sometimes just feel like more and more leaves are falling on your life? I wonder if this was what Solomon was talking about when he said:

I have seen all the things that are done under the sun; all of them are meaningless, a chasing after the wind.[6]

It almost seems as if Solomon knew about the easterly winds in the Perth foothills. But I digress! All too often I worry and procrastinate and then feel overwhelmed by all those things which press in on life. When I looked at the seemingly never-ending challenge of getting those leaves under control, I could easily become discouraged. When I look at all the aspects of my life that require energy and attention, I can feel overwhelmed. But, and here is the odd thing, when I was out there raking the leaves, those feelings would go away. When I make a determined effort to get my life and its schedule in order, those feelings have no room to take root. At the end of the day, I think that God has been teaching me to trust him more. Here I was asking 'When will the leaves stop falling?' God's response: 'Just go pick up the rake and get moving, Ian. Persevere, and trust me!'

Life sometimes throws curve balls at us. Good things and bad things happen to everyone. It is part of life, and sometimes we tend to over-emphasise what we see as bad things or unwelcome events in life. I have just done that. Those leaves were an irritant, not much more. Sure, I felt overwhelmed at times, and I grumbled 'when will it end?' as I went to fetch the rake, but deep down I knew that it was no big deal. I grumbled, but I knew that I could cope if this was the worst that life could throw at me. All I had to do was to just keep raking and eventually the leaves would cease to be an irritant. I just had to persevere.

The happy times and the times of sorrow are part of the ups and downs of life – it is almost cyclic, and we all go through them. As we experience those vagaries of life and yes, the small irritants like autumn leaves, we need to remember the adage that we have seen before – This too shall pass! Persevere, keep moving forward as best you can, and the time will come when the wind changes. Those headwinds change and become tailwinds.

When I was teaching, I had a poster on the wall of my office which read 'It's difficult to soar with eagles when you work with turkeys.' It had a big picture of a turkey and was just a bit of light-hearted humour but, as you might imagine, it did not do a lot to endear me to my colleagues. Of course, turkeys cannot soar. Turkeys just waddle. In fact, not many birds can soar. Eagles are good at soaring because of the strength in their wings but many other birds cannot soar. Some are good gliders. Others just do a lot of flapping. Did you know that a hummingbird can flap its wings 70 times a second? Of course, it doesn't get far, but all that flapping does enable the hummingbird to hover and extract the nectar from flowers. Seems like a lot of flapping for a little bit of nectar if you ask me, but there you go. Hummingbirds need the nectar to survive, so they just keep on flapping until they get the job done – perseverance.

Birds that can glide, of course, cannot just glide, at least not indefinitely. They need to flap a bit too. I know a bit about gliding as I used to do some sailplane gliding. When the tow plane releases the glider (it is actually the glider which activates the release) the sailplane starts to glide. Basically, from then on, it's all downhill. It's a nice ride but unless you can find an updraft, a thermal, you will be constantly losing altitude. Soaring on a thermal is what the sailplane pilot dreams of, and the pilot is constantly searching for a thermal because that gives lift under the wings and gains altitude thus allowing the sailplane to then glide further. As the sailplane glides to lower altitudes the pilot starts searching for another thermal which will again give lift so that once more the sailplane can soar to a higher altitude. Of course, birds can compensate by flapping now and then. Sailplanes or gliders can't flap.

Do you sometimes feel that there are times in life when we are soaring, other times when we glide through life, and yet other times when we need to do a lot of flapping? Do you know that exhilarating feeling that comes from soaring like an eagle? Fortunately, many of us do have times in life when we are soaring, lifted by the Spirit, times when we are born up by God's power. The prophet Isaiah had something to say about this:

> *Those who wait on the LORD shall renew their strength; they will soar on wings like eagles, they will run and not grow weary, they will walk and not faint.*[7]

Don't you wish that life was always like soaring? I can tell you from my experience in sailplanes that soaring is much more fun than just gliding. It's exhilarating – it's breathtaking. What a ride! And, in the same way, soaring in the Spirit also gives that exhilarating and breathtaking experience. You all know that, right?

But there are times when you run out of thermals and then you must glide. Gliding might not be soaring, but it is still nice. I think it is a bit like the next part of that verse from Isaiah *'they shall run and not be weary'*. Gliding really doesn't take a lot of effort, it's not going to wear you out, and if you manage it properly it can take you a long way. Large parts of life are like that, I think. We know where we are going, we know that we will get there, and we know that Jesus will run (or glide) through the course with us. It's comfortable, even if it lacks the exhilaration of soaring.

But then come the times when you cannot soar, and you cannot glide any further. You come back to earth, hopefully back at the airfield from which you departed, and hopefully without too big a 'thud', and then you must walk. We are almost back to the turkey analogy here. This is the third condition that Isaiah describes; *'They shall walk and not faint.'* Walking can be tough, but sometimes that is all you can do. But walking is enough. At those times all you can do is keep putting one foot in front of the other and say 'I'm walking, God, I'm walking! I don't feel like I'm getting far, and I can't see the finish line, but I'll keep walking'.

In the sixth century BC, the Chinese philosopher Laozi wrote 'The longest journey begins with a single step'. That is all you need do. Just take that first step and then keep on plodding, just keep putting one foot in front of the other, until the next thermal comes along – persevere.

So, may you be able to persevere and have wonderful times when your autumn leaves are under control. May you experience many times of tailwinds and fewer headwinds. May you know the exhilaration of soaring, lifted by God's Spirit, for there is nothing like it. And when you need to flap a little to get through, may God put strength in your wings. And when you need to walk, may you know that walking is just fine, and that Jesus walks with you, every step of the way.

1. Luke 18:1-8
2. Luke 11:1-4
3. John 16:33
4. 2 Corinthians 12:7-9
5. 2 Corinthians 12:9
6. Ecclesiastes 1:14
7. Isaiah 40:31

Chapter 7
Encouragement

This book which you are holding in your hands right now, sets out to be an encouragement to you. What does it mean to encourage? What does it mean to be encouraged? And is it important to be encouraged? The apostle Paul makes the point in his letter to the church in Rome that we are all given different gifts and one of the gifts which he identifies in that passage of Scripture is the gift of giving encouragement.[1] In exhorting us, in that letter to the Roman church, to give encouragement to one another, Paul is specifically speaking within the Christian context of giving encouragement to Christian brothers and sisters. Christians are always in need of encouragement, but when Paul was writing to the church in Rome that need was critical, in particular because of the abhorrent persecution which they faced under the reign of the insane and deranged Emperor Nero. And so, Paul was exhorting those Christians to be of encouragement to one another in the face of that persecution. Although overt persecution or hatred toward Christians is still found in some parts of the world today, most of us do not experience it. Nonetheless, we all know that life can be difficult at times. We still all need encouragement.

Christians, however, are not the only ones capable of giving encouragement, although perhaps they do it in a special way. The point, though, is that the word 'encouragement' is not one restricted to the Christian lexicon. It is used, also, in the secular lexicon and I believe that the meaning is, in many ways, common to both. It is reasonable, therefore, to examine the original Greek word which Paul used when he spoke of encouragement.

The word which Paul used when speaking of encouragement is the Greek word *paraklēsis (παράκλησις)*, a noun which carries the meaning of exhortation, encouragement, comfort, or 'a calling to one's side'. That last phrase, a calling to one's side, may seem a strange combination of words to some readers, although to the

Christian it carries the clear and unambiguous message of the Holy Spirit coming alongside us to encourage, exhort, and to give comfort. That, indeed, is why the Holy Spirit is sometimes called the *Paraclete*, because in the Christian context it is the Holy Spirit and/or other messengers sent by the Holy Spirit who come alongside us to exhort and to encourage. Later in this chapter we will certainly be taking a much more in-depth look at the person of the Holy Spirit in that role.

But, as we have noted, Christians are not the only ones who give, and receive, encouragement. I have many non-Christian friends who, at times, have been a source of great encouragement to me in different ways, and I thank them for that.

Everybody likes to be encouraged. Even more than that, everybody *needs* to be encouraged. I related in an earlier chapter the time of my sister's illness and death, a dark time during which I desperately needed encouragement. Part of the problem was the timing; I was a recent arrival in a new city, and I had no close friends in that city or indeed on that side of the country, I had not established myself at a local church, and I felt that there was nobody to whom I could turn.

I had withdrawn into my own little cocoon of pain and suffering, I had turned inward, and I could see nobody that I could bring alongside myself to strengthen me, to encourage me. I was, in fact, behaving like an echidna. Echidnas are native Australian medium-sized solitary animals covered with sharp spikes. Superficially, they resemble other spiny mammals such as hedgehogs and porcupines. When they are peacefully waddling along, the echidna's sharp spikes are laid flat against its body, but when threatened they immediately respond by curling into a tight foetal position, like a ball, with all spikes raised. In this position the echidna is saying 'This is my defensive posture! Stay away from me! Touch me at your peril!' It is the natural defensive posture of the echidna, and of we humans.

The other part of the problem was that I was neglecting the power and the role of the Holy Spirit in my life. I had turned to God in prayer, as I have told in an earlier chapter, but truth be known I think that I was probably not open to the encouragement of the Holy Spirit. Locked away and self-obsessed in that personal cocoon of suffering I had forgotten that the Holy Spirit was there to comfort and to encourage me. Without encouragement, suffering becomes all-consuming, the possibility of positive outcomes appears unlikely, we turn inwards towards our own suffering, and our will to persevere flounders. Without encouragement we begin to question God; does he care about us, and does he even exist?

Now, given that I had so abjectly failed to listen to and to respond to the voice of the Holy Spirit during that time of suffering and pain, I am aware that it will seem hypocritical of me to now extol the love, the importance, the power and the authority of the Holy Spirit, but God out of his grace has reminded me of his great love for me, and even that has been through the Spirit himself, and has called on me to tell you through my writing of the wonderful Counsellor who has been sent to live with us, to guide us, to comfort us, to encourage us, and to be even much, much more than that to us. Writing this may, indeed, be part of that healing process which God is performing in me.

So, let me tell you about the Great Encourager, the Holy Spirit. He has many roles. Yes, 'He!' The Holy Spirit is a *person* not some intangible and ethereal spirit. Not a theory, not even a celestial spirit, but the third person of the Trinity, the Spirit of God living within all believers; a living person intimately known and acting within the lives of Christians. Some Christians, and some Christian churches it must be said, are uncomfortable with the presence of the Holy Spirit and try to put him on a lower pedestal than God the Father, and Jesus the Son. Some churches even hope that he will stay away, allowing them to get on with their own impoverished and badly diluted form of church life. Some totally neglect the ministry of the Holy Spirit, believing that it is appropriate, and better, to concentrate on worship of the Father and the Son. But the Holy Spirit is the very Spirit of God and in every way is united with and equal to the Father and the Son. He was there, within the godhead, before creation. An important part of the inbuilt role of all three is to exalt the other two. Some will dispute that description of the Holy Spirit for it is a sad reality that the Holy Spirit is the least understood entity of the triune God, even by many Christians.

Furthermore, the Holy Spirit is the very continuation of the ministry of Christ. Can you imagine yourself as part of that small group of disciples in the upper room just a few hours before Jesus' arrest? I try to put myself into that picture and I try to imagine being there when Jesus said that he would be leaving us but that he would send another advocate to help us. I think that I would have been crying out, 'No, Lord! Don't go! Stay with us! We don't want another replacement, we want you! We *need* you!' Perhaps some of the disciples did say things like that or perhaps, at least, they thought it.

And, in a similar way, I think also of the years that I spent as a schoolteacher, and particularly of the three occasions during those years when the school Principal had retired. We will be getting a new Principal, I thought. It will be a time of uncertainty as we find our new direction. I wonder what he will be like. Will he be as good as the old Principal that we are losing? Will I be able to work with him? We always want to hold onto what we know and value.

But when Jesus spoke of leaving the disciples, and us, and of sending another advocate to be with us, he was promising much more than just an unknown change. Look carefully at his words.

> *And I will ask the Father, and he will give you another advocate to help you and be with you forever — the Spirit of truth.*[2]

That word 'another' which Jesus used was a word which meant 'another identical one' or 'another with the same characteristics'. This other advocate, the Holy Spirit, which God sent to help us, and to be with us forever, was one with Jesus in every way, not some lesser version of our Lord, but one with the same power as Jesus, the same love as Jesus, the same knowledge and grace as Jesus, and one sent for the very purpose of continuing the ministry of Jesus among us forever.

I know that I cannot do justice to all the roles of the Holy Spirit in our lives – my writing is not that good, and my human understanding falls well short of a full understanding of God. But it is opportune, I believe, to look at some of the roles which the Holy Spirit fulfils.

The Holy Spirit:

Exalts Jesus

I have stated earlier that, in part, the purpose of God the Father, Jesus the Son, and the Holy Spirit of God, is to exalt each other. Speaking of the Holy Spirit, Jesus said:

> *He will glorify me because it is from me that he will receive what he will make known to you.*[3]

Thus, the primary purpose of the Holy Spirit is to lift and to glorify the name of Jesus, and to prompt us to worship Him.

Convicts us

The Holy Spirit convicts unbelievers of their sins and reminds those of us who are already believers that at times, too often, we too still sin. At such times, the nudging of the Holy Spirit speaks to us through our conscience to make us aware of sin in our life, to draw us into confession of those sins, and to thereby bring us back into communion with Jesus.

Converts us

The Holy Spirit is the transformer. He is the agent of our conversion. It is the Holy Spirit who opens our hearts and brings us to the point of knowing that we need God's saving grace. And, when we come to Jesus in faith, trusting him for the forgiveness of our sins and for the salvation of God, it is the Holy Spirit who opens our heart and then dwells within us, filling us with the confidence and knowledge of God's love. Do you remember that wonderful and amazing feeling you had, that rush of adrenalin, that joy that you felt within yourself when you first came to Jesus in faith? That was the Holy Spirit transforming you and taking up residence in your life. And the Holy Spirit is not an optional extra. He is part of the package that comes at the moment of conversion, and without whom there would be no conversion. It can also be said that the Holy Spirit puts his seal on us, and through our fruits and the transformation of our lives he marks us as ones who belong to God.

Pours out God's love upon our lives

It is the Holy Spirit who tells us and assures us of God's love for us and pours it out upon our lives. I have known, perhaps all my life, that God loves me but there are times when the knowledge of that love goes to a whole new level. The moment of my coming to the Lord, the time of my conversion, was one such occasion. That is as you would expect, but there have been other times when, for no particular reason, I have just known, I have felt it in my bones, that I am loved by God with a love which is just beyond words. I cannot explain why those times come upon me, but that it is the Holy Spirit pouring out God's love upon me I have no doubt. I know that this is the action that Paul wrote about to the church in Rome:

> *God has poured out his love into our hearts by the Holy Spirit, whom he has given us.*[4]

Guides us

The Holy Spirit is a counsellor and a guide, who provides us with guidance in our daily lives. Jesus said:

But when he, the Spirit of truth, comes, he will guide you into all the truth.[5]

As Christians we have within us the Holy Spirit who is available to guide us in the paths of God and to keep us living in obedience to God. We need that guidance, moment by moment. We just need to make sure that we listen to it.

Teaches us

Jesus told his disciples:

The Holy Spirit, whom the Father will send in my name, will teach you all things and will remind you of everything I have said to you.[6]

As we open and study the Bible, God's word, the Holy Spirit enables us to understand what has been written there for us. He, the Holy Spirit, then guides us in the application of it in our daily lives. That is why I find it so helpful, almost imperative, that before turning to the Bible I pray that my thoughts and meditations on God's word will be guided by the Holy Spirit.

Empowers and Emboldens us

Having worked to make the Word of God clear to us, the Holy Spirit then empowers us to be bold in telling others of Jesus, and in sharing our faith with the world. A wonderful example of this is given to us in the book of Acts, Chapter 9, when a disciple named Ananias was spoken to by the Holy Spirit and told to go and minister to Saul, later to be named Paul. Ananias was reluctant to go, and with good reason, for Saul had made a reputation for himself by persecuting the believers and trying to wipe out this new religious movement called Christianity. But Ananias was then encouraged and emboldened by the Holy Spirit to go to Saul, to lay hands upon him, and to say:

> *Brother Saul, the Lord Jesus, who appeared to you on the road as you were coming here has sent me so that you may see again and be filled with the Holy Spirit.*[7]

That moment was, of course, the moment of conversion for Saul/Paul who then went on to become God's chosen instrument to proclaim the name of Jesus to the Gentiles and to their kings. But it took an act of significant courage on the part of Ananias and it was the Holy Spirit which gave him that courage. The Holy Spirit will do the same for us today when we go out to share our faith with the world.

Comforts and Reassures us

The Holy Spirit reassures us, as believers, that we are God's own children. Have you ever had doubts? Most of us have. And have you been reassured, perhaps through prayer, perhaps through reading scripture, or perhaps by the counsel of a Christian friend? That reassurance has come to you from the Holy Spirit. Paul, writing to the church in Rome, in Romans Chapter 8, perhaps one of the most beautiful chapters in all scripture, writes *'For those who are led by the Spirit of God are the children of God'*[8] and then goes on to say that *'The Spirit himself testifies with our spirit that we are God's children'*.[9] In other words, Paul is saying, it is the Holy Spirit which speaks to us and continually convinces and reassures us that we are part of God's family. The Holy Spirit is God's comfort to us.

Prays for us

This, to me, is one of the greatest gifts of God; that his Holy Spirit prays *for* us and *with* us – that the Spirit prays on our behalf. Most of us have probably encountered times when we just do not know how to pray, we just do not know what we can say to God. Sometimes we try, and our words are stumbling disjointed parts of sentences, but we know that even at those times the Holy Spirit prays on our behalf, and his prayers are perfect because they are actually from God, and to God. The apostle Paul wrote, again in that 8th chapter of the letter to the church in Rome:

> *The Spirit helps us in our weakness. We do not know what we ought to pray for, but the Spirit himself intercedes for us through wordless groans. And he who searches our hearts knows the mind of the Spirit, because the Spirit intercedes for God's people in accordance with the will of God.*[10]

How amazing is that? Don't ever think that your prayers are inarticulate or inadequate because you just can't find the right words, because even if your prayers are nothing more than wordless groans the Holy Spirit is there praying prayers on your behalf with prayers which are the perfect will of God - *'the Spirit himself intercedes for us through wordless groans'*. Have you ever groaned in prayer, with groans that are just too deep to put into words? Many (most) of us have probably been there. I've groaned, I've shouted, I've screamed, I've cried, I've uttered short phrases, like 'Where are you?' and 'Help me!', and I have weakly stuttered in my helplessness saying 'God, I don't know how to pray'. But take heart, be encouraged, because the Spirit is right there praying for you, and he *does* know how to pray, and he *does* know what to pray for!

Encourages us

I am sure that the Holy Spirit ministers in many other ways which I have not mentioned here, but let me mention just one more, and I have left this role of the Spirit until last because it is an integral part of the primary focus of this book – encouragement.

The Holy Spirit encourages us in so many ways that I am hesitant to start listing them here for I know that I will only scratch the surface. We can be, and often are, encouraged through reading the scriptures and that is one of the reasons we should regularly spend time in God's Word. We can be encouraged through prayer, through spending time with God and listening for his voice of love, assurance and guidance which comes to us through the Spirit. We can be encouraged through reading quality Christian literature, by listening to gospel music and by listening to the sermons and homilies through which God speaks to us. One of the most common ways in which the Holy Spirit encourages us is by sending others to us with messages from God. A person who has the spiritual gift of encouragement, whether it be spoken encouragement or written encouragement, is specifically given that gift for the uplifting and encouraging of others. And when we do that, whenever we allow the Spirit to speak through us to encourage others, God is glorified. I'd like to look, here, at a couple of people whose lives have been greatly used by the Holy Spirit to bring encouragement to others.

Perhaps the best-known Biblical example of one used by God to encourage others is a man whose actual name was Joseph, although the apostles called him by a different name. They thought it more appropriate to call him Barnabas because the name Barnabas means 'son of encouragement'.[11] What a testament to the life calling of this man, that others would nickname him 'the son of encouragement!' Wherever we find Barnabas mentioned in the New Testament, we find him encouraging others to love one another and, through their ministry, to be more energetic and more effective in telling the Good News. When the early church was understandably wary of accepting Paul because of his recent persecution of the church, it was Barnabas who came alongside the newly converted Paul and encouraged the church to accept him as a brother in Christ.[12] Barnabas accompanied and encouraged Paul on some of Paul's missionary journeys and we find Paul and Barnabas both encouraging new converts, Jews and Gentiles, to hold fast to their faith; to *'continue in the grace of God'*.[13]

Sometime later, Barnabas and Paul had something of a falling-out, but we find that the root cause of that disagreement was the very fact that Barnabas wanted to encourage another. Paul had wanted to revisit the churches which they had previously established in the area that was referred to as Asia-Minor, which was in fact the region of present-day Turkey. Barnabas was keen to go, but he wanted to take Mark along with them. Paul, however, was having nothing of that because Mark had deserted them in Pamphylia on a previous missionary journey and Paul would not trust Mark again. The writer of the book of Acts, Luke, writes that *'They* [Paul and Barnabas] *had such a sharp disagreement that they parted company'*[14] (words in brackets added by the author). Paul then took Silas as his missionary partner and departed, but Barnabas took Mark and sailed for Cyprus. Fundamentally, this disagreement and parting of ways arose because Barnabas wanted to encourage Mark and to give him a second chance, thereby drawing him back into ministry and into the service of Christ. This was the way of Barnabas – 'the son of encouragement.'

Let me tell you about another more recent son of encouragement. The late Ron Robertson was a wonderful though humble man of God, well known in the Baptist denomination in Australia. I knew Ron well, having come to know him through my friendships with his three daughters, friendships which endure today. I fondly remember sitting in the sunshine with Ron and his wife Nancy in the stand at the West Australian Cricket Ground in Perth and chatting all day while we watched a test match between Australia and England. Ron was a real cricket tragic. I, on the other hand, must confess that I was more interested in the chat than the cricket. Ron was a great man to listen to. His work and his roles within the Baptist denomination in Australia were so numerous and varied that one could easily write a book about his service to God, and perhaps one day somebody will do that. This is not the place for that book, so I will just pick out a few notable examples of Ron's service to the Lord.

Ron was the first full time Secretary of the NSW Baptist Homes Trust and he served 27 years as the Chief Executive Officer of that organisation. He was a gifted speaker and frequently travelled around the state of NSW speaking to churches about the work of the Baptist Homes Trust. In his home church Ron had a calling to teach and encourage young people, serving as a Sunday School Teacher, Sunday School Superintendent, and leader of the 'Christian Endeavour' youth group. There were many more roles, too many to mention, but I remember Ron as the voice of encouragement. I experienced it personally, and I saw first-hand the passionate encouragement which he gave to his children, his grandchildren, and his great grandchildren.

For many years Ron wrote a regular column which was published in *The Australian Baptist*, a denominational newsletter. Always, without fail, Ron's column was a message of encouragement in the Christian life, and here is the point – Ron used the totally appropriate penname of 'Barnabas'. Ron, too, was a 'son of encouragement'.

Do We Entertain Angels?

Sometimes we are encouraged by ones who we do not even know, ones who have been sent to us by the Holy Spirit, specifically to encourage us. When my mind turns to this matter, I am reminded of the words written by the writer of the book of Hebrews in the New Testament:

> *Do not forget to show hospitality to strangers, for by so doing some people have shown hospitality to angels without knowing it.*[15]

Some of today's biblical scholars debate the intended use of the word 'angels' in this verse of scripture and question whether it really does apply to celestial beings, perhaps one of the worshiping angels around the throne of God. The word used in the original Greek was ángelos (ἄγγελος) which can be translated meaning an angel, a heavenly spirit, or a messenger. Some of today's biblical scholars argue that the use of the translated word 'angels' should be taken as a metaphorical reference to visitors, perhaps visitors who one does not know, because they just may be someone that God has sent to you with a message, or to help you in some way.

I want to tell you about one more man who greatly encouraged me, one who I believe was sent to me by the Holy Spirit, and I do not even know his name. I mentioned in an earlier chapter that I had experienced two of those very difficult and painful journeys through the Valley of Baka although when I mentioned that I chose to withhold relating the second of those experiences to you. This is the place to tell that story.

For more than twenty years I had suffered from an inability to control my emotions. In short, I would cry at the drop of a hat. When it first started happening it was very infrequent. I remember the first instance sometime in the mid-1970s, and then it may have been a year, or the best part of a year, before it happened again. Over time it became more and more frequent until, by the early 2000s, it was happening several times a day. There was no identifiable trigger for these emotional meltdowns. It could happen when I was watching a television commercial. It could happen when I was just sitting in the couch and relaxing without a thought in my mind. It could happen when I was driving. It could happen when someone simply said 'Hello' to me. Sometimes I could feel that it was about to happen and if I were with people on those occasions, wherever I was, I would get up and rush out. As you can imagine, it became the source of much embarrassment. My doctor told me that I was suffering from depression and, notwithstanding the fact that I disagreed with him, at his urging I did try a large range of anti-depressant medications, all to no avail.

I remember the first time that I met the pastor at the church which I had started attending. He would become a remarkably close friend, a spiritual mentor, and a great source of encouragement to me, but on that first occasion when he just came up to me and said 'Hi. I don't think we've met. My name is Michael' I just dissolved into tears. And I don't mean that I became a bit emotional and my eyes got misty. I am talking here about sobbing uncontrollably and not being able to say a word. Michael asked if he could come and visit me later that week, so I wrote down my address and phone number for him. He came to visit a few days later and I was able to talk on that occasion. It was the start of a wonderful friendship which endures today.

On another occasion I had arrived early for church and I was just sitting in the pews waiting for the service to begin. I had not spoken to anyone. Because I had arrived so early there was not even any music playing and I do not even remember what I had been thinking about at the time. There were no emotional triggers but suddenly I was in tears and I had to get up and rush out. Lexi, a good friend, saw this happen and she came to me to see if she could help, and when she asked, 'What's the matter?' I had to say 'I don't know. I have no idea. I just have to get out of here and go home.' It was the morning after that incident that I decided to go back to my doctor and to demand some action, and when he started to tell me that I was suffering from depression I became quite forceful with him and said 'The only thing that I am depressed about is that you keep telling me I am depressed. I want to be referred to a specialist neurologist.'

An appointment was made for me to see a specialist neurologist at one of Perth's prominent hospitals – a doctor who turned out to be a lady of about 45 years of age. She ordered a series of tests including an MRI brain scan and when she got the results of those tests I was called to go and see her again. 'Well,' she said, 'You've lost about 7% of the front left quadrant of your brain.' I thought to myself, 'Well that figures. I'm always losing things.' She went on to say that it is the front left quadrant of the brain which controls our emotions and I started to think that it was good that we were at last getting some definitive diagnosis. 'Well, what can we do about it?' I asked, at which point she totally crushed my spirits by saying, 'We can't do anything about it. We cannot make your brain grow back, and we cannot stop it from deteriorating further. It will get worse. You will get dementia.' She had some long name for it which I cannot accurately remember; something like 'involuntary degenerative hyper-emotionality disorder'. I left feeling totally deflated and without any sense of a future.

I decided that maybe she knew what she was talking about, but I certainly didn't like her manner, so I visited my GP again and asked for another referral, in order to get a second opinion. An appointment was made with another specialist neurologist working on the other side of the city but, as is often the case when making appointments to see specialists, there was a wait of several months until he could see me. I just made a note of the date and put it on the fridge door so that I would not forget the appointment.

When the time for the appointment drew near, I looked at the date and was somewhat surprised to see that the appointment would be on a Saturday morning. I thought it strange that a specialist physician would be seeing patients on a Saturday, so much so that I called his rooms to confirm the date. 'Yes, that's right', his secretary said, 'The doctor sometimes sees patients on a Saturday and your appointment is at 11am next Saturday'. So, on the day of the appointment I set out to go to his rooms which were in a nice and rather upmarket part of town. It turned out that this neurologist worked out of a nice old colonial style cottage which had been beautifully renovated – the type of cottage which has a hallway straight through the middle of the building with rooms leading off the hallway to the left and to the right – typical Australian colonial architecture. The first room on the left was the secretary's office and she told me that the waiting room was up the hallway on the left-hand side. The doctor would not be long, she said.

The waiting room was a very nicely appointed room – nice artwork on the walls, an open fireplace (but no fire burning), and two rows of seats along two opposite walls so that the seats were facing each other. The room was also empty. I was the only one there. Now, you might understand that I was feeling very anxious. I already had one disconcerting diagnosis and this doctor might very well confirm that diagnosis and leave me facing a bleak future. I had brought along the films and clinical reports from the earlier MRI scan and felt it was likely that this doctor would look at those and come to the same conclusion as had the first neurologist. I sat down and tried to browse through a magazine, but my anxiety continued to grow.

About 15 minutes after I had arrived, another couple came to the waiting room and sat down against the opposite wall, facing me – a youngish man who I thought was probably in his mid to late 20s, and a woman who I took to be his mother. They were both well dressed, looked affluent as people from this part of town would be, and the woman was an elegant and attractive woman. But my attention was drawn to the young man because he was looking directly at me and he had, quite simply, the most beautiful smile that I had ever seen. He was literally beaming, and he was beaming at *me!* I remember thinking 'That young guy has got it made! Affluent, very handsome, and that amazing smile!' And then he spoke to me, and as soon as he spoke it became obvious that he had profoundly serious brain injury. His speech was so badly slurred that I found it almost impossible to understand what he was saying.

Now, I must confess that I don't handle situations like that very well. My normal response would probably be to smile and then to hide behind a magazine, but there was something totally captivating about this young man. Perhaps it was that smile! Whatever it was, I put down the magazine and walked across the room to sit down next to him and we started to talk. I am a real introvert, and I would normally never have done that, but something was drawing me to him. Conversation was difficult, and I had to ask him to repeat most things two or three times before I understood what he was saying, but I found myself warming to him moment by moment. The woman did not say anything, but she was watching us, and she too was smiling. I asked the young man if he had been in an accident and, with difficulty, he said 'I was runned over'. He was showing no scars from the accident, and he had walked quite normally when entering the room. There were no outward signs that he had been in an accident, just the brain damage. We talked about all manner of things – I remember that he told me that he liked the boots that I was wearing. For my part,

I no longer cared whether the doctor was running late – I really did not want this to end.

We talked for about twenty minutes and that amazing smile never left his face. He was just glowing with friendliness. I was enjoying talking with him so much that my anxiety had totally subsided, and then the strangest thing happened. The woman (was she his mother?), suddenly said 'Well, we'd better be going', the young man shook my hand and struggled to say, 'You take care', and then they just got up and left. They didn't see the doctor! What just happened? Who were they? Where had they come from? Why were they there? Where had they now gone? I still do not know the answer to those questions. They had gone and I was left alone once again in an empty waiting room, but the experience had settled my anxious heart.

A few moments later the doctor called me into his room to see what he could do for me. He looked at the previous MRI scans and reports and he asked a lot of questions. At one point he commented that I appeared to be distracted and that I really was not focussed our conversation. He asked whether I commonly had difficulty concentrating on things, and on engaging in conversation. It seemed that he thought my lack of attention was part of the symptoms that I had come to see him about, so I decided to tell him what had just happened in the waiting room. He just looked at me very quizzically. He didn't say 'Well, that couldn't have happened' or even 'Well, I don't know who that could have been,' but the way he was looking at me left me in no doubt that he had no idea what I was talking about. I asked whether he thought I was crazy, and he replied 'No, I don't think you're crazy. I think you have just experienced something, but I'm not sure what that was'.

Incidentally, his diagnosis was much more positive. 'Yes', he said, 'there has been some brain shrinkage' (well, at least that sounds better than saying that I had *lost* it!), 'but we can control the emotions and stop further deterioration with medication'. I had to try a few medications until we hit on the right combination, but the problem is now totally under control and I feel great.

I thank God for that doctor, for his caring diagnosis and for the encouragement that he gave me. But far more than that, I thank God for that young man in the waiting room. I would love to be able to talk further with him and I wish that I could find him again. But I have no way of finding him. I don't think that I am meant to find him. He was there for me at the time when the Holy Spirit knew that I really needed encouragement.

Friends with whom I have shared this story have often asked, 'Do you think that he was an angel?' Well, perhaps. I do believe that God, through the Holy Spirit, does send messengers to us; messengers who might be celestial beings or who might be one of our fellow humans, a person with whom we might or might not be acquainted, one whom God has sent with a particular message for us – messages of instruction, messages of correction or of rebuke, messages of comfort, messages of reassurance, and messages of encouragement.

So, was that young man in the waiting room an angel? I have no idea. He may have been just some young man who, for reasons that I still do not understand, was there when I needed him – or he may, indeed, have been an angel. Whether he was an angel or not, I do not know. But that he was a messenger sent from God, through the Holy Spirit, to encourage me and to minister to me in a time of need, I have no doubt. He was certainly an angel to me!

1.	Romans 12:8	8.	Romans 8:14
2.	John 14:16	9.	Romans 8:16
3.	John 16:14	10.	Romans 8:26-27
4.	Romans 5:5	11.	Acts 4:36
5.	John 16:13	12.	Acts 9:27
6.	John 14:26	13.	Acts 13:43
7.	Acts 9:17	14.	Acts 15:39
		15.	Hebrews 13:2

Chapter 8
Choose How to Live

Life, as we have discovered, can be like riding a roller-coaster. Joy and sorrows, laughter and tears, harmony and conflict, health and illness, triumphs and disappointments, anxiety and contentment; the list could go on. Some would add to that list, blessing and curse, but blessing and curse are in quite a different category for, whereas all the other conditions listed above are part of the natural rhythms of life in this fallen world, I believe that blessings and curses are things that you can choose.

Way back in the Old Testament, when the Israelites were wandering in the wilderness on their way from Egypt to the Promised Land, Moses set before them a choice of blessings or curses. Moses had spent most of his life exhorting the Israelites to hold fast to God and to live in obedience to his laws and commands. Through the voice of Moses, God would present the Israelites with a choice – blessings or curses. They would receive the blessings of God, wonderful awesome blessings, if they loved God and lived in obedience to his laws. They would have the curses poured out upon them, dreadful curses, if they turned away from God and worshiped other gods. Why would anybody want the curses when they could have the wonderful blessings? And yet, God knew that the Israelites would turn away from him for he told Moses:

I know what they are disposed to do, even before I bring them into the land I have promised them on oath.[1]

Moses, knowing that he was about to die, wanted above all else to do everything in his power to ensure that the Israelites held fast to God and received the blessings. He told the Israelites:

This day, I call heaven and earth as witnesses against you that I have set before you life and death, blessings and curses. Now choose life, so that you and your children may live.[2]

We all face the same choice, blessings or curses, life or death. We choose – God delivers. So, it is a simple choice, right? We choose to love God, to place our faith in his goodness and to live our lives in obedience to his will, and in return we will be blessed with a rosy life, a long life, happiness, contentment, good health, a perfect marriage, perfect children, and financial prosperity, right? No, it doesn't work like that though some Christians believe it to be so and, dare I say it, some churches teach that it is so. Some churches, even today, base their beliefs and practices on what has been called "prosperity theology."

Prosperity theology, sometimes referred to as the prosperity gospel, maintains that God always wants the very best for us, which is true, but the proponents of prosperity theology then extend that by making our relationship with God into a contract through which, if we have faith in God, make monetary donations to the mission of spreading the gospel, and outwardly proclaim that Jesus is Lord of our lives, then God will deliver to us security, good health, happiness and prosperity. And, if you don't receive those things from God, so the doctrine goes, well your faith was just not strong enough. I related in an early chapter the incident of a Christian couple coming to me following the death of my sister to tell me that it would not have happened had her faith been stronger - prosperity theology.

I sometimes wonder how adherents to prosperity theology rationalise the millions of Christians who live in abject poverty and poor health, caused by malnutrition and unsanitary living conditions in many poor and undeveloped countries around the world, countries like Mali, Mozambique, Ethiopia, Haiti, and many others. Are they saying that Christians living in those countries live in poverty because their faith is not strong enough? Even writing those words makes my anger burn within me because I firmly believe that the reason for such poverty has more to do with the fact that those countries are saddled with crippling foreign debt which was accumulated by wealthy western nations selling goods and services (often military hardware) on credit and with interest rates which would mean that the developing countries would never be able to repay even the interest much less the capital debt. In developing countries such debt enslaves millions of people in never ending poverty. Don't you dare tell me that those Christian brothers and sisters of ours live in poverty because their faith is not strong enough! They suffer in poverty largely because of our greed and avarice, and the abolition of such debt should be one of the prime focuses of the praying heart of the church today.

Prosperity theology has figured prominently in televangelism and has often expressed itself in emotive and undignified appeals for cash donations which, more than anything else, appeared to be used for the enrichment of the evangelists and for the building of huge and self-indulgent edifices wrongly purporting to be to the Glory of God, televangelism cathedrals and the like. It was, and remains, irresponsible, unscriptural, and exploitative of the poor.

So, if we are going to dismiss prosperity theology, and I can find no words to dismiss it strongly enough, then what are we to make of the fact that we choose to love God, to live in accordance with his will and his laws as best we can, and to put our faith in his Son Jesus Christ for the forgiveness of our sins, and yet still find ourselves beset by the burdens of sorrows, trials and conflicts which can, at times, batter us and push us all over the emotional spectrum, even to the depths of despair? What we conclude from that, the only thing that we can conclude from that, is that, as stated earlier, we live in a fallen world, in a world of our own making and of our own choices. It wasn't meant to be so and that it breaks the heart of God that it is so.

We have pondered in previous chapters the promise of Jesus that in this world we will have troubles. I am not sure about you but there are times, when those troubles beset me, that I find myself thinking 'Well, that's a promise that I could have done without.' But Jesus, of course, was only reminding us of the reality of the world in which we have chosen to live, and he also gave us many other positive and beautiful promises of life with him, none more so than the words '*I have come that they may have life, and that they may have it more abundantly*'.³ We'll come back to those beautiful words shortly.

When the Israelites had moved into the Promised Land and had driven out many (though not all) of the Canaanites we find their leader, now Joshua, putting before them the same choice of blessings and curses, almost echoing Moses' words. The eastern tribes were about to return to their families living east of the Jordan, taking with them their share of the plunder of silver, gold, and large herds of livestock. And to them Joshua said:

> *Be very careful, to keep the commandment and the law that Moses the servant of the LORD gave to you; to walk in all His ways, to obey His commands, to hold fast to Him and to serve Him with all your heart and all your soul.*⁴

Joshua went on to thank them for their service, blessed them and said farewell to them, and then, in his last exhortation to them, Joshua put before them a choice, much as Moses had done:

> *If serving the LORD seems undesirable to you, then choose for yourselves this day whom you will serve, whether the gods your forefathers served beyond the river, or the gods of the Amorites in whose land you are living. But as for me and my household, we will serve the LORD.*⁵

You see, we do have a choice. God loves us and he wants us to love him in return and to live by his law. But we do not have to do that. This is where the choice comes in – we can say 'No!'

But if we do face the same choice which the Israelites faced when Moses and Joshua put before them the choice of blessings or curses, and if we have committed our lives to following Jesus and to living in obedience to God's laws as best we can, then we might at times feel a little short-changed if the blessings don't appear to be flowing our way. We might also look around us and see others living without any respect for God and for his laws, living idolatrous lives, corrupt business lives, immoral lives, and yet appearing to be receiving those blessings which we, in our misguided ignorance, think should have been ours – success, prosperity, good health and long lives. What is going on? Have the blessings and the curses been directed to the wrong people?

I think of the numerous women in my extended family who have suffered long agonising deaths because of breast cancer. Some of them died far too young, one at the age of 32 leaving behind two infant children. Those women were not sinless, to be sure, but they were good God-fearing Christian women who sought to live righteous lives. Contrast that with somebody like Joseph Stalin, responsible for the torturous death of up to twenty million people and who died in his bed at 74 years of age and with a smile on his face, and you begin to ask whether God's justice has been misdirected.

But, in fact, God's final judgment has not yet been directed anywhere. It is held in abeyance because God's final judgment on each one of us, Christian and tyrant alike, comes at the end of time. It is not immediate. Stalin will have his day of judgment, and the righteous will have their day of judgment, and that is when the real blessings and curses will be distributed. One who has built a life of righteousness in this world, with God's help, will know the real blessing of life eternal in his presence when Jesus returns and establishes the Kingdom of Heaven on earth.

Although God's final judgment is held in abeyance until the return of Jesus that is not to say that in this life there are never any consequences for sin. Sometimes, as an act of discipline, God can and does remove his hand of grace in order that we might learn from that and correct our ways. Our God is a just God who hates sin and does sometimes discipline those whom he loves by withdrawing his hand of grace, for a season, and saying 'It pains me, but there are consequences for your sin. We are going to need to deal with that'. We do the same when there is need to discipline our own children. Indeed, any good and loving father, and God is the perfect loving Father, will find times when he needs to act in disciplining his own children even though it hurts him to do so.

There are many examples in scripture where God has disciplined those whom he loves, and who love Him. Think, for example, of the consequences visited upon David and Bathsheba because of their sin of adultery, and David's hand in organising the death of Bathsheba's husband, Uriah the Hittite. Yes, our God is a God who wants to forgive us and if we confess our sin before God, he will immediately forgive us. And David, when confronted with his sins by the prophet Nathan, did immediately confess his sins and was forgiven by God.[6] That does not mean that there were to be no consequences for those confessed sins. For David and Bathsheba there were terrible consequences – the death of an innocent child, and within their family there would be upheaval, betrayal, rapes, and murder down through the generations.

Another clear example of God removing his hand of blessing and grace because of sin is revealed in the Assyrian and Babylonian exiles of the Israelites. For centuries, God had raised up prophets to deliver his message of warning to the Israelites, only to see his prophets mistreated and ignored. Amos warned the Israelites of the northern kingdom that God was giving them ample warning, and that if they did not turn away from the worship of foreign gods and turn back to him, then they would be conquered and taken into exile by the Assyrians. Amos alludes to future political events that God would use to deliver his judgment on the northern kingdom of Israel[7] and numerous times he speaks of the coming deportation into exile of the people and their corrupt leaders[8]. Deportation of conquered peoples was a standard practice by the Assyrians and later the Babylonians. Even at the eleventh hour, so to speak, God was still exhorting Israel to turn back to him in repentance and avoid his judgment. But the people would not respond and God's judgment, as prophesized by Amos, would be brought upon them. Most would be taken into exile by the Assyrians, and only a remnant remained in Israel.

The same warnings were issued to the southern kingdom of Judah, especially through the prophets Isaiah and Jeremiah, this time with warnings that conquest and exile would come at the hands of the even more ruthless Babylonians. Jeremiah, in delivering God's warning to Judah said:

> *The word that came to Jeremiah concerning all the people of Judah, in the fourth year of King Jehoiakim son of Josiah of Judah (that was the first year of King Nebuchadnezzar of Babylon), which the prophet Jeremiah spoke to all the people of Judah and all the inhabitants of Jerusalem: For twenty-three years, from the thirteenth year of King Josiah son of Amon of Judah, to this day, the word of the* LORD *has come to me, and I have spoken persistently to you, but you have not listened. And though the* LORD *persistently sent you all his servants the prophets, you have neither listened nor inclined your ears to hear when they said, "Turn now, every one of you, from your evil way and wicked doings, and you will remain upon the land that the* LORD *has given to you and your ancestors from of old and forever; do not go after other gods to serve and worship them, and do not provoke me to anger with the work of your hands. Then I will do you no harm." Yet you did not listen to me, says the* LORD, *and so you have provoked me to anger with the work of your hands to your own harm.*[9]

'*And so, you have provoked me to* anger' said the Lord God, thus withdrawing his hand of blessing and grace from the people whom he loved. In consequence, the entire kingdom, a nation believed to have been ordained by God himself, collapsed and the people were taken into 70 years of exile in Babylon. Centuries of prophetic warnings had fallen on deaf ears and God was left with no option but to visit this calamity upon the people whom he loved.

Yes, there are times when God, as a just and loving father, finds it necessary to visit punishment and suffering upon us as an act of discipline. It pains him to do it, and he does it with a broken heart, but at times, we leave him with no alternative. I have experienced times in my life when I know with absolute certainty that periods of pain and suffering have been the consequence of my sin, and I am sure that many readers will be able to relate to that in personal ways.

Notwithstanding that, it is also true that not all suffering is the result of our sin. The psalmist writes:

He does not treat us as our sins deserve or repay us according to our iniquities.[10]

If he did, we would all be living in perpetual misery and suffering, because we know that we cannot obey all of God's law all the time. God knows that too. It was for that reason that he sent his Son, Jesus, to die in our stead and to pay the cost of our sins, in order that we could be forgiven. We who are sinful and unworthy (and that is all of us) can choose to be redeemed by the blood of Christ and to be forgiven by the grace of God. We can choose whether to live condemned by the law, or whether to live under God's grace.

Does that mean that we who have been forgiven should, as the apostle Paul asked, *'continue in sin that grace may abound?'*[11] Some of my non-Christian friends ask a similar thing of me – 'So, if you're forgiven that means you can do anything now because you're forgiven?' No, of course it doesn't mean that! Yes, if we have accepted Jesus as Lord of our lives we are forgiven, all our sins are forgiven, past, present, and future, but God still wants and expects us to follow his paths and to live a life of righteousness in obedience to his laws. And the reason? For our own well-being! God wants us to have happy, rewarding and fulfilling lives. We were created to live righteous lives, in communion with God, and our lives function best when we do that. As for me, I cannot think of any other way in which I would want to live my life.

So, in the words of Moses and of Joshua, choose today how you will live your life. Now, that challenge of how you will choose to live your life operates on two levels. First, and most importantly, it applies to the choice which you will make concerning whether you will, or will not, accept God's forgiveness and his salvation offered through faith in his Son, Jesus Christ. This is the choice which will determine your life in all eternity; the choice between having the 'life in abundance' which Jesus spoke of, or a life of eternal sorrow and torment. Choose carefully!

We should look, here, at what Jesus was talking about when he made that wonderful promise of life in abundance. Jesus said:

The thief does not come except to steal, and to kill, and to destroy. I have come that they may have life, and that they may have it more abundantly.[12]

The thief that Jesus referred to is Satan. Satan comes only to steal our joy, to discourage us and to kill off our desire to live the life that Jesus gives us the moment that we accept him as our personal saviour. Jesus is not like that. Jesus comes not to steal, but to give, and the gift is life eternal and life in abundance.

Jesus was not talking about a long and healthy life in this world when he spoke of bringing life more abundantly. Abundant life in this context has nothing to do with length of life in this world. Neither has this 'abundant life' got anything to do with the accumulation of wealth and of nice material possessions. So, you've got a beautiful wife (or a handsome husband), you've got a nice family, you own your own home, a nice home in a nice area, you've filled it with nice possessions, you've put a couple of nice cars in the garage, you've sent the kids to the best schools and colleges, you've got a good bank balance and retirement funds all prepared. There is nothing wrong with that, provided you have shared your good fortune with those who are less fortunate. It is natural that we aspire to have material possessions which will make our life in this world more comfortable, but we should hold onto those things loosely, because they are not permanent. Abundant life *is* permanent, it *is* eternal. It has nothing to do with what we have or how successful we have been in life. That is the so-called 'good life', it is not 'abundant life'. For followers of Jesus, abundant life is not about what we have, or how long we might live on this earth. Abundant life is about what we get from Jesus – his joy, his confidence; his hope, and his orientation of the heart.

In short, 'abundance' has both a secular and a spiritual meaning. Before we became followers of Jesus, we were consumed by the desire to accumulate 'stuff'; things that were nice to have but that we didn't really need. But Paul tells us that when we come to Christ we become *'a new creation'*,[13] and when writing to the church in Rome, Paul reminds them that part of that 'new creation' is the transformation and renewal of our attitudes and of our minds:

And do not be conformed to this world but be transformed by the renewing of your mind.[14]

Real abundant life is living life with an abundance of the fruits of the Spirit; love, joy, peace, forbearance, kindness, goodness, faithfulness, gentleness, and self-control.[15]

What things are important in life to you? You can rest assured that Satan is not going to come and steal your 'stuff'. He knows that it holds little real value. He is after something much more valuable, your joy, your love of God, your peace. He wants your life, and your attitude. So, what is your attitude to life? What does it tell you about the things that are important in life to you?

I am reminded of an opportunity that I had, quite some years ago, to attend a program at one of the largest churches in Perth, Western Australia; a program promoted as *An Evening with Philip Yancey*. Philip Yancey is, of course, one of the most prolific writers of contemporary Christian literature in the world today, and I commend his work to you. On that occasion, when I heard him speak, Yancey told us of a television news broadcast in the Ukraine, and that in the Ukraine the news on television had a little square picture-in-picture, down in the bottom right-hand corner of the screen, where a woman related the news in sign language for the deaf. Perhaps these days, in the Ukraine, they have closed captions on modern televisions, but in the time which Philp Yancey was describing they relied on the sign language interpreter on the screen. Now, the newsreader, in the big picture, we were told, was saying 'The election result is now known, and the government has been re-elected with an increased majority', but what the woman in the small picture in the bottom right-hand corner was saying in sign language was 'They are announcing that the government has won the election. We all know that they are lying through their teeth and that the election was rigged. If you want to protest, go to the city square tomorrow morning.' The ensuing protests forced the government to hold new elections which led to a change of government, all because one woman had the courage to say 'Don't listen to him. They're lying through their teeth.'

Yancey then went on to tell us that, about a year earlier, he had been in a serious road accident. His car had skidded on icy roads and crashed off the side of the road, rolling down a steep ravine. When the ambulance crews got to the vehicle he was still in the car and his neck was broken. They were not exactly sure how bad his injuries were, but the prognosis was not good. He was told that he might fully recover after surgery and a long rehabilitation, that he might be confined to a wheelchair for the rest of his life or, in fact, that he might well die within the next 24 hours. And while they did further tests, for the next 8 hours, he was strapped to a flat board so that he could not move. And Yancey told us this: he said 'When I was strapped to that board for 8 hours, not knowing whether I would live or die, I didn't think about what my hair looked like. I didn't think about what kind of car I drive (it was being towed to the scrap yard anyway), I didn't think about my investments, or how many books I had sold that month. I thought about my family, those that I love, what I had done with my life, and whether I was ready to meet God.' Nothing focuses the mind like the thought of impending death and right at that moment, not knowing whether he would live or die, Philip Yancey thought about the things that are truly important.

You see, we are bombarded every day with news, advertising, images, and opinions that tell us that life is all about success. It is about finding a beautiful wife or a handsome husband, it's about your career, about how much money you've made, it's about your image, your possessions, your house, your car, your investments, which school you have sent your kids to. And in pursuit of that success, we force ourselves to work harder and harder, longer and longer, because the trappings of success are all-important. That is the big-picture, and it is projected to us constantly. Yancey would say 'Ignore the big picture. Look down here in the bottom right-hand corner. They're lying through their teeth!'

To single-mindedly pursue those trappings of success means to operate purely on a personal level, a self-indulgent level, a level which pursues only one's own goals, one's own plans, one's own desires, and which totally ignores what God has in store for our lives. Philip Yancey, I imagine, is an affluent man, but he knows that abundant life has nothing to do with abundant possessions. The 'abundant life' which Jesus spoke of is eternal life spent in his presence and it is given to us the moment that we accept Jesus Christ as our personal saviour. It has nothing to do with a long and prosperous life in this world. It has everything to do with the promise of a thoroughly joyful life and eternal life, starting now, spent in the presence of Jesus, the one who loves us like no other.

But, as has already been noted, that challenge of how we will choose to live our life, that choice with which we are confronted, also operates on another level – it operates on an attitudinal level in the here and now. It asks about the attitude with which you will face those troubles which Jesus promised would come along. And when that happens, when those huge troubles do come, will you choose to turn inwards, like the echidna, and perhaps throw a 'pity-me' party, or will you choose to hold fast to the encouraging words of Christ when he said '*But take heart! I have overcome the world*'[16] and to believe that this too will pass? That second attitude is not easy, and you know that at times I have failed that test. But that is the choice, and the challenge, that we face in times of adversity. Don't look to the way that I responded but look to those examples of which there are so many, where people have displayed the most amazingly positive attitudes and have acted magnificently in the face of true adversity.

I recently read *Tales from The Secret Annex* by Anne Frank. Many readers will know of Anne Frank, a young Jewish girl born in Germany in 1929 who together with her family had to flee the country of their birth in the face of growing antisemitism after Adolf Hitler came to power in Germany. The family set up home and business in Amsterdam, The Netherlands, only to find that the threat of Nazism followed them when Germany invaded and conquered The Netherlands in May 1940. With the help of his business partners, Otto Frank set up a hiding place in the annex of his firm at Prinsengracht 263, and there Anne and seven others hid from the Nazis for two years, having to maintain total silence during the day and living in constant fear of discovery. After more than two years in hiding the group was discovered by the Nazis and deported to concentration camps, from which Anne's father, Otto Frank, was the only one of the eight people to survive. After her death, and after the end of the war, the teenage Anne Frank became well known because of the diary she had written whilst in hiding, and no doubt many of my readers will have read *The Diary of Anne Frank*.

I don't know whether you can imagine life under those conditions. I find it difficult to imagine the strain that it must have put on their minds living there in that cramped annex for over two years, knowing that discovery meant a terrible death. And yet, when you read the writings of Anne Frank from that time, that terrible and dark time, what shines through is the positive attitude of that young girl. In *Tales from The Secret Annex*, Anne wrote:

> *How wonderful it is that no one has to wait but can start right now to gradually change the world! How wonderful it is that everyone, great and small, can immediately help to bring about justice by giving of themselves!*[7]

Where does that come from? How does a young girl living in hiding, in constant fear of discovery and death, find it within herself to express such positive thoughts? And we should remember that Anne Frank was not a Christian. She was a Jewish girl and as such she no doubt had a strong belief in God the Father, in Yahweh, but she did not have the promises of Jesus or the power of the Holy Spirit to strengthen, support and encourage her. The positive and optimistic expressions throughout her writing, I believe, come from an attitude towards life in our current circumstances which refuses to accept that current adversity will last forever. It is an attitude which says that being optimistic in troubled times is not just being foolishly naïve, and that looking for the best even in the darkest circumstances is to acknowledge that in this world we encounter not only deceit, betrayal and brutality, but also love, compassion, goodness, sacrifice, goodwill and generosity. My dad used to say to me 'If you look for the worst in this world, Ian, you will surely find it. Look for the best.' Anne Frank would agree.

Attitude is a choice, and the choice that you make will define you. Noam Chomsky, the famous American linguist, and philosopher is widely credited with having spoken, or written, about the attitudinal choice with which we are faced. I have been unable to trace the original source of this quote. I cannot find where Chomsky said it, or wrote it, although I have no doubt that it truly is a 'Chomsky quote', and it is certainly relevant here.

> *Optimism is a strategy for making a better future. Because unless you believe that the future can be better, it is unlikely you will step up and take responsibility for making it so. If you assume that there is no hope, you guarantee that there will be no hope. If you assume that there is an instinct for freedom, that there are opportunities to change things, there is a chance you may contribute to making a better world. That is your choice.* — Noam Chomsky

Dwelling on the worst that life has to offer destroys our capacity to do something about it, whereas choosing to emphasise the beauty of life gives us the impetus to act in a way which makes a difference in this world. Again, Anne Frank would agree.

We should not be focused upon how long we will live, for other than taking care of ourselves, keeping fit and eating the right foods we have no real way of influencing that. Generally, we do not get to choose how long we will live. We do get to choose *how* we will live. The way in which we choose to respond to all experiences in this life, the triumphs and the beatings, is directly influenced by that choice. We can choose to muddle through this fleeting life hoping that things might work out all right and that the world might get better, or we can take the initiative, with God's help, to make it so. We can choose to believe that we were put on this earth to live a life full of passion and purpose.

Anne Frank stated a universal truth when she wrote that every one of us 'can start right now to gradually change the world!'[18] Most people, and certainly all Christians, believe that this world should be a more ordered and just place, that they can make a difference in this world, and that our efforts to make this world a better place are not in vain. That belief is, in and of itself, a remarkable victory over the forces of darkness. And, in this we Christians have a great advantage because we do not struggle merely through our own human resources, but we are empowered by the Holy Spirit who works through us.

Optimism is a choice. Attitude is a choice. And, choosing to enjoy that 'abundant life' of which Jesus spoke is also a choice. We know that the promise of abundant life is not about the number of years that we will be given in this life, nor about the stuff that we might accumulate along the way, but that it is about eternal life in the presence of our Lord, starting now, and it is about a satisfying and meaningful purpose in this life. It is a life that we are continually growing into.

The apostle Peter wrote that we should 'grow in the grace and knowledge of our Lord and Saviour Jesus Christ'.[19] To 'grow' is a continual on-going process of leaning on our Lord who is also our teacher. It involves learning, failing, getting up again and seeking the guidance of the Holy Spirit so that we can get it right next time, and moving ahead with an optimism which is firmly rooted in God and is evidenced by the fruits of the Spirit – love, joy, peace, patience, kindness, goodness, faithfulness, gentleness and self-control.[20] This is the abundant life which is given to us the moment we accept Jesus Christ as Lord of our lives; abundant joy and purpose in this life and eternally abundant life in the Kingdom which is our sure and certain inheritance. So, let us choose to live our lives in the abundant life which Jesus gives to us. Every day we should be striving, with the empowerment of the Holy Spirit, to ensure that this day we will be the best person that we can be.

Each morning, when we rise, let us live a life in which we refuse to be discouraged by difficult circumstances or by our own perceived failures, for those circumstances and attitudes are given to us by the evil one, the 'joy stealer.' To ignore and to overcome those difficult circumstances can be exceedingly difficult, as I well know. But with the power of the Holy Spirit, we can and must move forward. To live a life discouraged by such things is almost a slap in the face of God, a refusal to live the abundant life that Jesus offers us. Instead, let us live life knowing that Jesus Christ has given us life in abundance. Let us be encouraged by that, let us thank God for that wonderful promise, and let us live our lives accordingly.

1. Deuteronomy 31:21
2. Deuteronomy 30:19
3. John 10:10 (NKJV)
4. Joshua 22:5
5. Joshua 24:15
6. 2 Samuel 12:13
7. Amos 6:14
8. Amos 4:3, 5:5, 5:27 & 7:17
9. Jeremiah 25:1-7
10. Psalm 103:10
11. Romans 6:1
12. John 10:10
13. 2 Corinthians 5:17
14. Romans 12:2
15. Galatians 5:22-23
16. John 16:33
17. Frank, A. *Tales from The Secret Annex* p.87
18. Frank, A. Ibid
19. 2 Peter 3:18
20. Galatians 5:22-23

Chapter 9
When the World Changes

November 2019. It came out of the city of Wuhan, in China, from a live animal marketplace, or was it an escapee from a biological research laboratory? We were not greatly worried, after all, we are not Chinese. The first infection outside of China is thought to have been in Thailand, but still few of us worried because we are not Thais either. Infections followed rapidly in South Korea, Japan, Malaysia, and India before seemingly escalating exponentially in Iran, and then ravaging Western Europe, Italy, France, Spain, Germany, The Netherlands, and Britain. No country, anywhere, was exempt. The Trans-Atlantic jump of the virus brought devastation to the United States of America, and to other nations of the Americas. It was rapidly infecting people and causing an increasing number of deaths all over the world; in Scandinavia, in Eastern European countries, in African countries, throughout the Middle East and, of course, it found its way to our country, Australia. They called it Covid-19, and at the time of writing, as we wait, hope, and pray for a vaccine, it is undeniable that our world has changed in so many ways. It might never be the same again.

And as our world sinks further into distress, and at times into despair, as we accustom ourselves to the so-called 'new normal' of social distancing, as we take on face masks and accept them as the new must-have apparel (even fashion-statements for some) we ask ourselves, 'Why has this happened to us? What have we done to deserve this?' Different factions have different answers to those questions.

There are the conspiracy theorists. I don't give any credence to their claims, but they would have us believe that the virus was deliberately released by the Chinese government as a means of crippling the western economies, particularly that of the United States of America. 'After all,' they point out, 'China, the source of the virus, has suffered far less, both in terms of a health crisis and of an economic crisis, than most of the western world. If it was the objective of the Chinese government to facilitate the ascension of their own state to a position of economic supremacy over the West, then they have been largely successful.' Some conspiracy theorists point to the fact that China is now almost Covid-free, whilst infection numbers in the rest of the world are still high, and in most cases still climbing. Given China's huge population, and the fact that it was the source of the pandemic outbreak, that causes some people to suggest that China had some covert hand in the spread of the pandemic. Others conspiracy theorists go even further and suggest that such action on the part of the Chinese government was but the second stage of a combined Sino-Russian strategy to weaken the West both politically and economically. The first stage, they suggest, was Russian interference in the 2016 US election aimed at bringing into office the Trump administration – first weaken them structurally by giving them an egomaniacal and self-obsessed political leadership, and then hit their economy! The warming relationship between China and Russia is also cited as evidence of this conspiracy theory. I reiterate that I, personally, give no credence to these conspiracy theories.

Some Christian groups, too, have their own answer to our questions; 'It's God's retribution on an evil and unrepented world' they cry from the sidelines. 'It's a sign that The End is near, and that God is about to pass judgment on a sinful world. Listen now, and repent, before it's too late.' Some other Christians would simply reassure us; 'Don't worry! Stay calm! God is in control. Trust him.'

Then there are the 'pandemic deniers', those who claim that the pandemic is being blown out of all proportion by governments and by the media. Just yesterday I heard a man say, 'more people are killed, in our city every day in traffic accidents, than those who die each day of Covid-19.' Well – yes maybe, or maybe not – I am not familiar with the statistics of people killed on our roads each day. But a traffic accident is something that I may be able to see coming, that I can at least try to avert. That is quite different to knowing that the person who I stand close to in the supermarket may give me an unseen illness, which he or she might not even know that they have, that can kill me within a week. A traffic accident has some inherent element of control. Not so with this pandemic. Face masks and social distancing notwithstanding, there is no way that we can control the random and unseen attack of the Coronavirus. So, who is in control? Is anyone in control?

Governments around the world try to assure us that they are in control. They bring daily briefings to our television screens, but very few of us are convinced that any government has the crisis totally under control. In my country we are given daily figures for new infections, and for national daily death totals, with a breakdown of figures on a state-by-state basis, and we tune in every morning hopeful that there may be indications that things are improving. Some days it appears that things are improving, some days not. Few of us have confidence in the governments of the world to control both the threat to public health as well as the economic devastation caused by this pandemic. If social and business lockdowns are continued, and strengthened, then the world faces company and personal bankruptcies on an unprecedented scale, soaring unemployment, greater levels of mental illnesses within the community, the breakdown of marriages and societal structures, general malaise and increasing suicide rates. If lockdown restrictions are eased, on the other hand, and businesses begin to reopen, then infection numbers and the number of deaths soar again. The debate, in almost every country, swings from the economic imperative to the health imperative, and back again. And all along we mourn and weep for those around us who become ill, or perhaps die; we weep because often we cannot even hold their hand or say goodbye to them as they die, and our own mental health deteriorates as we come to terms with our inability to do anything about it. The toll is not only on those who succumb to the virus, but also on those of us who are forced to impotently watch on, in anguish, from within the gloom and the depression of a so-called 'Covid-safe lockdown.'

And it is not only our country which is suffering and groaning through this pandemic. We, the world's people, are all in this together. Indeed many, if not most countries are in a far worse position than we are in Australia. Most countries, like ours, vacillate between saving lives and reopening the economy, and fail in both endeavours. Whilst every country, without exception, is suffering from the onslaught of the Coronavirus, it is clear that the country most severely impacted by the virus is the United States of America, with, at the time of writing, infection numbers approaching 30 million, and the number of deaths approaching half a million. Really though, quoting statistics here serves little purpose for the statistics continue to rise exponentially, and those numbers quoted above will be out of date by tomorrow – by next week the numbers will be exponentially higher. I know that I should keep politics out of this discussion, but I cannot help myself. I have to say that I believe that, in large part, the extremely high statistics in the USA are not coincidental to the fact that as the virus took hold within the USA, the nation was led by a man incapable of responding to such a crisis, indeed a man totally unqualified to lead what was once the world's major superpower. Even some of Donald Trump's own family have come out and described him as a self-obsessed and egocentric man who is totally incapable of managing the affairs of state.

Comedians around the world made a living from unmercifully lampooning and ridiculing Trump. The man was an obvious target for comedians and, if the consequences for the United States of America had not been so critical and far-reaching, it would indeed have been laughable. Trump clearly suffered, and still suffers, from an immeasurable degree of egocentricity which manifests itself only in exhibitionism and grandstanding. It could be a mental illness. His Administration was irresponsible governance – governance by Twitter! This is the man, after all, who said 'Of course we are finding more cases [of Covid-19] than any other country! That's because we are doing far more testing, so I've asked the health authorities not to do so much testing,' and 'It [Covid-19] will go away, it will just disappear – Believe me!' And you ask why, around the world, respect for the USA has fallen? Really?

For most of my lifetime, in times of crisis, the Western world has tended to look to the USA for leadership. No longer. Trump has made the United States of America an irrelevance. Perhaps the USA will, in time, be able to regain its honour and respect within the international community. I hope that they do, for we need a strong America, but it will take wise and prudent national leadership, and it will take time – the Trump legacy in America has not been swept away by the election of a new Administration.

Where is God in all of this?
At times like these many people, even unbelievers, can be heard to ask, 'Where is God in all of this?', 'Why has God allowed this to happen?' and 'If God is in control why does he not just make it stop?' Those are germane questions – after all, we ourselves are harassed and helpless and we, or at least many of us, know that we must reach beyond ourselves to find deliverance from this pandemic.

One of my favourite words in all Scripture, one word that assures me that I have something or someone to turn to, or to return to, one word that describes the very nature of God and which answers those questions above, is the word 'compassion'. The Old Testament Jews knew that their God was a God of compassion – more than seventy times the Old Testament scriptures assured them of that.

> *'Though the mountains be shaken, and the hills be removed, yet my unfailing love for you will not be shaken nor my covenant of peace be removed,' says the LORD, who has compassion on you.*[1]

And when God incarnate stepped down into this world in the person of Jesus Christ, the gospels record on many occasions that Jesus, God made flesh, was filled with compassion for us:

> *When he [Jesus] saw the crowds, he had compassion upon them, because they were harassed and helpless, like sheep without a shepherd.*[2]

Our God is a God who, by his very nature, is a God of compassion. But what does that word mean? Does it mean that God empathises with us in our troubles? Does it mean that he feels sorry for us, that he sympathises with us? Well, yes, but if that is all that it means then I am not sure that is good enough for me. I am not sure that sympathy and empathy alone make God someone that I can turn to in times of trouble. Sympathy goes only so far.

Fortunately, to ascribe a meaning of empathy or sympathy to the word 'compassion' is doing nothing more than making the most superficial scratch into the meaning of the word. As we have seen in an earlier chapter (p. 25), the word 'compassion' comes from the Latin word, *cumpassio*, which is itself a compound of two Latin words, *passio* meaning 'to suffer', and *cum* meaning 'with'. To say, then, that our God is a God of compassion means that he is right there in the front line, alongside us, suffering with us, groaning with us in our travails, sharing our fears and our tears, knowing our feelings of helplessness and hopelessness. That, on one level, might lead us to question whether God really is 'in control', as we often are told – it may even lead some to conclude that God, too, is as weak and helpless as we ourselves are in such situations. Well, yes, and no.

I say 'yes and no' because we have a tendency to want our God to be all powerful, which he is, and we want him to exercise that power, to *display* that he has everything under control. We tend to want visible signs of his power and we want to be able to *see* that he is in control. But God does not always work that way. Sometimes God stands alongside us, with compassion, and says to us 'my grace is enough for you.'

In several places throughout this book, we have come back to the reality in which we live, the reality that declares that bad things happen to good people because we live in a fallen world, a world of our own making. And the Coronavirus pandemic is one of the very worst of those bad things to have happened, certainly the worst in living memory. We live in a world which prompted Jesus to tell his disciples '*In this world, you will have trouble.*'³ That's a promise, a guarantee; you *will* have trouble, because you are living here, in exile, in this fallen world. We were exiled from God's perfect kingdom and placed here because of the sin of all mankind; because God in his holiness cannot allow sin to be present in his perfect kingdom, the Kingdom of Heaven. That raises the question; if God is not weak and helpless, if God is not only compassionate but is also omnipotent, why does he not just change this fallen world, rid it of all its ills, including the present pandemic? Why does an omnipotent God of compassion not simply turn this world into a utopian kingdom of love and peace, where we can all live without pain, sorrow, and the myriad of troubles that we experience day by day?

Well, the short answer is that we, the people of this world, have shown that we are not very good at living in love and peace and, because of that, this world in which we live, in which we are exiled, still has sin within it. If God were to snap his fingers and make this world perfect it would, in effect, mean taking us back into the Kingdom of Heaven, from which we have been exiled, and that would reintroduce sin into God's Kingdom, thus defeating the purpose of our exile in the first place. It would also mean that the substitutional sacrifice of Jesus Christ on Calvary's cross was worthless and unnecessary – a God who was willing to fix the world and bring us back into the kingdom simply by snapping his fingers would not have needed to send his own Son to die in our stead.

The good news, however, is that God is at work, preparing us, and the world, for readmission to the Kingdom of Heaven. Yes, it often seems like one small step forward and several steps backwards, and that is our fault. We are the ones holding God back and delaying this process. (Readers who are interested in exploring further the promised reunification of our world and the Kingdom of Heaven might like to read my earlier book, *'The Mustard Seed – God's Promise of New Creation'*.) But God *is* in control of that reunification process and eventually we *will* be brought back into his perfect kingdom. In the meantime, the fact that we must live in this fallen world with all its ills and trials, breaks the heart of God. And so, he joins us in our suffering, he groans, and he weeps with us – he has compassion upon us.

There are numerous references in Scripture where groaning is mentioned. God heard his people, the Israelites, groaning as they endured slavery in Egypt.[4] David wrote in the Psalms, '*I am worn out from my groaning*'[5] and then goes on to acknowledge that the LORD heard his groaning and his tears and responded.[6] But perhaps the best-known reference to our groaning is in Paul's letter to the church in Rome, where he writes:

> *We know that the whole creation has been groaning as in the pains of childbirth right up to the present time. Not only so, but we ourselves, who have the first fruits of the Spirit, groan inwardly as we wait eagerly for our adoption to sonship, the redemption of our bodies.*[7]

Not only that, says Paul, but:

> *In the same way, the Spirit helps us in our weakness. We do not know what we ought to pray for, but the Spirit himself intercedes for us through wordless groans.*[8]

There it is! God, through his Holy Spirit, shares in the suffering of the world, identifies with our pain, hears our groaning, understands how eagerly we await the full realisation of the Kingdom of Heaven on earth, and himself '*intercedes for us through wordless groans*'. We, and God the Holy Spirit, groan together in wordless groans, groans that are just too deep to put into words.

And, right now, the world is groaning in ways much deeper than most of us can ever remember. We don't always know what we should pray for, indeed there are times when we feel that we just don't know how to pray, but God hears our wordless groans because the Spirit is there groaning with us, and for us. *That* is where God is in this pandemic. God is right here, suffering and groaning with us. Perhaps a more pertinent question, and one with a far different answer, would be 'Where is the church in this pandemic?'

Where is the Church in all of this?

Church pews are empty. There is nothing that we can do about that, for governments and local authorities have mandated that churches, and other institutions where public gatherings would normally be held, must cease holding gatherings such as church worship services. And, in fact, I am okay with that!

What is the true function of the church anyway? Why does the church exist? Is its function to hold weekly meetings, or is its function to serve and to worship God through service to his people, the wider community? Yes, coming together for corporate prayer and for corporate worship is a vital and indispensable part of church life. Make no mistake, I do not want to detract from that, but I put it to you that if the church claims its existence solely by holding weekly meetings then it runs the risk of becoming little more than a Sunday social club.

Many churches, almost all, have responded to the legislated closure of church meetings by going online. Each week, emails are sent to those who would normally be attending their church services, giving an e-link that those people can follow to hear and watch podcasts of their pastor delivering his weekly sermon. 'Oh, and please make your tithes and offerings online.' It is almost business as usual – perhaps it is even a little easier than business as usual. Many churches have interpreted the ban on public gatherings to mean that the church must stop being a church. Well, perhaps it never really was a church in the first place – perhaps it was just the

Sunday social club. How will churches respond when restrictions on gatherings are lifted? Will they just go back to doing church the way they did pre-pandemic?

Recently the pastor at the church that I used to attend sent out an email requesting feedback. There was only one question; 'What is it about the way that we used to do church, which you most miss?' I thought about that question for a long time. I really considered it deeply, and especially in respect to that particular church, and I concluded that my answer would have to be 'Nothing! There is absolutely nothing about the way that we used to do church that I really miss. Nothing at all!' To me that is a sad indictment on that church which shall remain unnamed in these pages, though I acknowledge that some would argue that it is a sad indictment on me. They may be right.

Now, I am not suggesting that your church is necessarily the same as the church that I have just mentioned. Nor am I suggesting that all churches are like that. Inasmuch as my response to that request for feedback is applicable to your church, only you and your fellow worshipers can say. But I do believe that a great many of our churches are similar, in varying degrees, to the Sunday social club.

The previous few paragraphs have been difficult for me to write. Believe me, I am not a 'church-basher', and I prayed long and hard before deciding not to delete those words from the text. I am still not totally comfortable with having written those paragraphs, but after prayer I have chosen to let them stand. And so now, having written it, I have concluded that my initial question, 'Where is the Church in all of this?', was perhaps the wrong question to begin with. So, now I must ask a slightly different question.

Where *should* the Church be in all of this?

Although we are unable to conduct normal worship services the church must not retreat to a position of isolation behind closed doors and podcasts. Social distancing might mean discontinuing corporate worship services, but it does not mean ignoring the desperate needs of others. The church must remain connected both within the church community and, more importantly, with the broader community. And the church doors must be open; open like never before. In times when the community is suffering widespread pain and suffering, the church must be a beacon of hope, help and deliverance. People in the community are hurting in an unprecedented way. Unemployment has soared, and will go higher, people are stretched financially, many are likely to be cutting back on meals and other necessities. People are frightened and many are experiencing mental health issues because of the hardships they are facing and simply because being in lockdown, particularly for people who live alone, is inherently depressing. Large part of the church's vocation must be caring for such people and helping to meet their needs. But sitting back and hoping that people will watch the church podcasts is not good enough. The church needs to be proactive rather than reactive. The church needs to be going out into the community and finding those people who are in need, rather than waiting for them to come to the church for help because, for many of them, and to the church's shame, the church is the last place that they expect to find that help. By seeking out those in need and by engaging with the needs of the surrounding community in this pandemic the church will find itself fulfilling perhaps its most fundamental role; that of serving those whom Jesus referred to as *'the least of these.'* [9]

And, if we are missing communal worship at this time, then we can find our worship through our obedience to Jesus' command that we love one another. The highest form of worship is not sharing in communal singing with hands raised, though I am not saying that is not a valid form of worship. But no, the highest form of worship is obedience to God's will and to Jesus' command that we love and serve one another. The role of the church is to serve, and to serve with humility. Jesus, himself, showed us the clearest example of such love and service when, at the gathering which we know as 'the last supper', he took off his outer clothing, wrapped a towel around his waist and washed the feet of his disciples,[10] placing himself clearly in the position of servant. *That* is where the church should be during this pandemic. Actually, of course, the church should always be there, but particularly when the world is hurting as it is right now. Obedience – service - worship. It is worship *through* service – service to one another, and service to the community.

So, what can we do? How do we find those in need? That is not always as easy as it might seem. It can be confusing to work out how we can help and, though I hate to say it, that may be because we, the church, are further removed from the community than we would like to think. But with prayerful consideration we can draw up a list of initiatives through which the church, and we as individuals, can reach out in service to the community. I am going to offer a list of possible initiatives, but it is not an exhaustive list. You, the reader, can add to it or can delete some of the listed initiatives where they are clearly not relevant to your community.

Be engaged:
* Contact local government offices and ask where you can help. They will be acutely aware of community needs.
* Many local community organisations who work with the most vulnerable, need your help to deliver their services. (not only 'physical' deliveries as in driving but perhaps in other ways, e.g. by manning telephone call centres, etc.)
* Canvass your church members. Many of them will know of families in the community who are struggling and who need help in various ways.
* Some may be able to manufacture face masks for distribution within the community. I know one lady who has set up her own home production line and has produced thousands of washable and re-usable masks. Perhaps you can do something similar in cooperation with other members of the church congregation.
* Those with medical experience, for example retired nurses, can offer practical medical help and advice.
* Some may be able to provide and distribute masks and small bottles of hand sanitiser.

* Be particularly aware of friends and neighbours who you suspect may be struggling with mental health issues, depression, anxiety, panic disorders, etc. You may know that some of them struggle with maintaining their mental health. They may have discussed it with you in the past, which likely means that they are willing and open to talking to you about it now. Reach out to them, share your time with them chatting over coffee, and take them small gifts. Let them know that you are there and that you want to help them.
* Stay in touch with your neighbourhood, especially the elderly and those who live alone. Make cold phone calls and ask 'How are you doing? Can I help in any way?' Some of them may need help with shopping for their essentials or they may need transport to appointments, etc. Or maybe they just need a word of comfort and of encouragement. Perhaps they just need to know that someone cares about them.
* Churches can open emergency pantries to which members of the church congregation can donate canned food and other non-perishable items and can work closely with local support organisations to distribute the food to the most vulnerable. Food baskets or food vouchers can be prepared for distribution.
* Help by volunteering as a delivery driver or by driving to support those with disability who need help to access their essential services.
* School teachers, or retired teachers, can offer to assist their neighbours with home schooling during school closures.

Add your own dot-points to the above list. And pray. Prayer, of course, should be a given.

Pray
* Pray for your neighbours, for your community, for your state, for your nation, and for the world.

* Pray for our frontline medical professionals, for nurses, doctors, hospital orderlies and admin staff, paramedics, and ambulance drivers. Pray that they will be kept safe.
* Pray for those throughout the world who are working in research to find a vaccine.
* Pray for our political leaders; pray that they will be given wisdom, that they will value people over the economy and that they will listen to the vulnerable over those with powerful self-interests.
* Pray that where national leaders engage only in grandstanding and egocentric exhibitionism that God will raise up responsible and competent national leaders, men and women whose first concern will be the well-being of their people rather than their own image.
* Pray that in nations where there are deep divides, especially in the United States of America, that God will raise up men and women who are healers; men and women who can begin unifying the nation once more.

After the pandemic?

By the time you read this book, the pandemic may be over. A vaccine may have been found. I hope and pray that it is so, but I fear that we may yet have to live with this virus for quite some time. Even when we do have a vaccine, we are going to need to learn how to live with the virus which will almost certainly continue to live within the community. Whether the pandemic is over or not, the point was made at the beginning of this chapter that our world has changed in many ways, and that it might never be the same again. Our immediate reaction to that statement is that such change is bad, that it is undesirable. But not all changes have been bad. The pandemic has forced us to reassess many of our priorities and perhaps, in some cases, that is for the better. We must hope and pray that the realignment of some of those priorities will continue post-pandemic.

Have you noticed that during this period of pandemic, extremist religious terrorism which had been called 'part of the new-norm' has not reared its ugly head? Even the invective of cross-culture and cross-religion name calling has been largely absent.

There have been other positive changes to have come out of this realignment of priorities, too. In isolation we have been forced (and perhaps we needed to be forced) to spend more time with our families, and particularly to spend quality time with our children, sharing with them, reading with them, playing with them, loving them more. Many people have discovered that they can work from home, and may continue to do so post-pandemic which, because they are not commuting to the office, not only has given them more time to spend with their families but at the same time has resulted in lower vehicular emissions and a cleaner environment. We may miss the convenience and the pleasure of international travel but, for now at least, the vastly reduced air traffic has also given our environment a chance to take a fresh breath of cleaner air, although clearly international air travel will recommence when the pandemic is over. Furthermore, because our priorities have shifted, we have caught glimpses of a society in which some people are willing to disrupt their own routines and to make sacrifices for the well-being of others. Will this continue post-pandemic, or will we revert to business as normal?

In this pandemic I see an opportunity; an invitation to transform ourselves and our community into a more selfless, loving, and self-sacrificing group of people who share in one another's burdens, financially, socially, emotionally, and practically. We have the opportunity here to become a more compassionate society, one which will come out of this coronavirus pandemic reborn as a better and more unified world than that which we have been used to. Let us pray that it will be so; and let us worship through service to make it so.

1. Isaiah 54:10 2. Matthew 9:36 3 John 16:33
4. Exodus 2:24 5. Psalm 6:6 6. Psalm 68:8-10
7. Romans 8:22-23 8. Romans 8:26 9. Matthew 25:40 10. John 3:3-5

Chapter 10
Leave the World a Better Place

Bumper stickers seem to have disappeared in recent years, probably in recent decades. And I suspect that is largely because modern cars really do not have bumper bars – most just have some plastic body moulding which would not survive any bump. But I used to like reading bumper stickers, in fact if I saw one that I liked I would write it down. I never had a bumper sticker on my own car, but I have quite a collection written down. One of my favourites from that collection is 'Lord, make me the kind of man that my dog thinks I am!' But, again, I digress. I had wanted to commence this chapter with a quote which is commonly attributed to Mahatma Gandhi, and which used to be quite a common bumper sticker – 'Be the Change that You Want to See in the World.'

Whether Gandhi ever used those words is debatable. In the 1989, 30 July edition, *The Yale Book of Quotations* cites The Los Angeles Times as stating that 'According to the Gandhi Institute for Nonviolence, this has not been traced in Gandhi's writings.' There is, in fact, no persuasive documentary evidence which should lead us to attribute this precise quotation to Mahatma Gandhi. Like many quotable quotes, words often appear to have been paraphrased from other words which people did use. In this case it may have been paraphrased from Gandhi's words below:

> *If we could change ourselves, the tendencies in the world would also change. As a man changes his nature, so does the attitude of the world change towards him. This is the divine mystery supreme. A wonderful thing it is and the source of our happiness. We need not wait to see what others do.*
> - Mahatma Gandhi

Many people, today, recognise that quotation, 'Be the Change that You Want to See in the World', and regardless of its origins, it inspires people to want to do something worthwhile with their lives. Most of us want to know that our life has mattered in some way, that we have made a difference. But how do we measure that? Many people speak of leaving a legacy, or at least wanting to leave a legacy. For some people that legacy is found in their children, and in their grandchildren, those that they leave behind to carry on the family name and values. I, myself, have no children, but I can understand the desire that people have to leave part of themselves behind. Others, especially those approaching the winter of their lives, as I am, tend to look back over their lives and to reflect on what they have achieved, not in terms of monetary or financial accumulation, although some do that, but more often in terms of what they have given to others and what influence they may have had on their community, or even on the world community.

What do we mean when we speak of leaving a legacy? Ask half a dozen people and I suspect you might get half a dozen different answers. Some want their name to be remembered for putting their stamp on future generations. Some want their name to be associated with great achievements. Poets want their words remembered, and some of the great poems are remembered although often we struggle to remember the name of the poet. Some of the great classical music composers are remembered by name, Mozart, Tchaikovsky, Beethoven, Bach and so on, but for most of the more recent or contemporary composers it is their musical compositions rather than their names which are remembered. Writers want their books to remain in print, with their name on the front cover, of course. Sports persons and those well known in popular culture sign autographs thus proliferating their names, at least until those who hold the autographs tire of them, lose interest, and toss them out. In short, for many people, leaving a legacy means having their name remembered. To me, that seems a little narcissistic, and that is why I draw back a little from the use of those words, 'leave a legacy'.

But the term, 'leave a legacy' is in such common usage now that I am almost forced to use it, though I want to disassociate that term from the desire to have one's name remembered. I have no problem with the concept of living a life which will leave the world a better place for our having passed through it; indeed, I applaud that, and I hope that my life, too, will not have been in vain, that it will in some small measure leave this world a better place when I am summoned out of it. But it is the tendency to associate a legacy with a name which seems, to me, to be a bit self-serving and egocentric.

Leaving a legacy, I believe, is not measured in terms of how long one's name will be remembered, but rather in terms of the impact that one's life has had on others. It has little to do with leaving a monetary inheritance for your descendants, or philanthropic bequeaths to social welfare causes. It will be measured in how you have lived your life, how you have displayed your virtues and your character in the day-to-day embodiment of your missional life.

My aunt, Phyllis, was an inspirational Christian lady whose life and lifestyle was built solidly on her faith in Jesus Christ. And I am sure that when the Lord summoned her out of this world, he would have said to her 'Well done, Phyllis. A life well lived.' She didn't leave me any property or a monetary inheritance – she had little to leave, but she did leave me with something far more valuable than any of those things – she left a Godly legacy. I must admit that I ignored that legacy for many years, for more than half my life in fact, but that legacy never died and when I was ready to turn back to God it was at least in part that legacy which drew me back and reminded me that I was coming home. Aunt Phyllis was a much-loved aunt and during my youth she probably had more spiritual influence on me than any other person. She died at a relatively young age (57), and I have in my home a small plaque which she had owned. That small plaque which sat in her home and which now sits in my living room, carries the following poem:

> I shall pass through this world but once.
> Any good therefore that I can do
> Or any kindness that I can show
> To a fellow creature
> Let me do it now.
> Let me not defer nor neglect it
> For I shall not pass this way again.

Interestingly, from my perspective, that small plaque does not record the name of the poet. Research shows that some attribute that poem to one Stephen Grellet, a Quaker missionary who reportedly escaped the French guillotine and fled to America during the time of the French revolution, although this attribution seems to be widely disputed. But does it matter? Who knows who wrote the poem? Indeed, who cares? It is the poem itself that is the legacy. It is the poem that inspires, not the name of the poet. I remember fondly my Aunt Phyllis who owned that small plaque, though I am sure that the next generation in our family will not remember her name. What I remember about her most of all is that she actively lived out the words of that poem.

Some time ago, perhaps ten years ago, I was doing some family ancestry research and because I was passing through the small country town where I had lived in my youth, I decided to go to the local History House and see if I could find Aunt Phyllis' obituary in the newspaper files. The History House office was staffed by an incredibly old lady, probably well into her 80s or perhaps even in her 90s. Aunt Phyllis had died in 1973, but when I told this very old lady that I was searching for the obituary of my aunt, Phyllis Schoupp, she paused and then said 'Oh, my goodness! You must be Phyllis' nephew. I remember her so well after all these years. She was the finest lady I ever knew.' Aunt Phyllis touched this world which she passed through, she inspired others and she impacted the lives of those she met – she made a difference even if few will remember her name.

Like most people, I want to feel that my life has mattered and that I have made a difference, but I really don't care whether or not my name is remembered, which is probably just as well because I am quite sure that my name will not be long remembered. Within a couple of generations, I will be a faceless name in the family records, or perhaps a faded photograph in the family album. People will probably look through that album and say, 'I have no idea who that is', and I am okay with that, I have no problem with that.

Recently when I was walking in Melbourne City, I could not help noticing the significant number of statues and monuments dedicated to the memory of prominent people from our nation's history. On a nice patch of lawn alongside St Paul's Cathedral in Swanston Street, is an imposing statue of Matthew Flinders, standing statuesquely in his small boat, being pushed ashore by other seamen. Now, I know who Matthew Flinders was, (I was schooled in a time when we were taught such things) and I know what he did that warranted him being memorialised in stone. But I strongly suspect that most of those from younger generations would not even know the name of Matthew Flinders. I would be absolutely astounded if one in a hundred of those passing by could tell you anything at all about him. His monument, and his name, are today little more than a picturesque resting place for pigeons and a receptacle for their droppings. History is fickle and names are generally, although not always, fleeting! It is vanity and hubris to desire to have one's name remembered. It is commendable and honourable to impact this world in a positive way through the quality of one's life.

The words 'in a positive way' are critical words in that last sentence for there can be no doubting that the quality of one's life can impact the world for good or for ill. Since 1927, *Time* magazine has issued an annual cover bearing the image of the person it has chosen as 'Person of the Year'. It is not a popularity contest. *Time* bases its choices on the person that has had the greatest impact on the world that year, be it for good or for ill. In 2016 Time's Person of the Year was Donald Trump. Adolf Hitler was Person of the

Year in 1938. Joseph Stalin, one of the most ruthless authoritarians in history, was Person of the Year in 1939 and again in 1942. Surprisingly, or perhaps not so surprisingly, those whose lives have impacted the world for good are somewhat more difficult to find. *Time* seems less inclined to choose those who might come to mind as people of virtue and righteousness. Mother Theresa, for example, was never Person of the Year. Mahama Gandhi was (1930), Martin Luther King was (1963), and Nelson Mandela was (1993) but, by and large, *Time* seems to choose world leaders, influential politicians, military people, sports persons, etc. rather than those whose personal lifestyles have actually impacted the world for good. *Time*, of course, was not around in the days of Jesus of Nazareth, but I suspect that had *Time* been around in those days, it would be rather unlikely that Jesus would have been chosen as Person of the Year. Perhaps King Herod may have been chosen, perhaps Emperor Tiberius, perhaps even Pontius Pilate, but it seems likely that the itinerant rabbi who would have more impact on the world for good than any other person in history would probably have been overlooked.

And how about you and me? You probably should not expect to see your face gracing the cover of *Time*. Most of us will never reach the lofty heights of recognition shared by those villains and heroes listed above. Most of us will fall somewhere in the middle, among the vast breadth of humanity. But we do get to choose where we will stand, on which side of that line dividing good and ill, just as Adolf Hitler chose his side of the line and Mother Theresa chose hers. We all get to choose our side of the line and the way the quality of our lives will impact on the world.

For many people, I suspect, when contemplating the influence that they have had on the world around them, it is their career(s) which first come to mind. Perhaps you are thinking about that now, as you read these words. Did your career leave your footprints upon those you worked with and upon those you met through that career? That can be a formidable and unnerving question to ask yourself – I know, I have just done it. Over the course of my life, I have had several careers, perhaps the main career was the twenty-five years that I taught high school. Some three and a half thousand high school students passed through my classroom during those years. The minimum number of lessons that each of those students spent in my classroom was 5 lessons per week, those in the senior years had 7 lessons per week (a 40-week academic year). The minimum length of time spent in my classroom was 4 years (800 lessons), some up to 6 years (1,360 lessons). I calculate the number of individual lessons to be the number of lessons multiplied by the number of students in the classroom, that is to say that one lesson taught to a classroom of thirty students is equal to thirty individual lessons. Now, my calculations might not be accurate (I did not teach mathematics!), but I calculate that over those twenty-five years I taught a total approaching 3 million individual lessons.

That absolutely staggered me when I did those calculations and even today, in my retirement years, I often think about those thousands of young lives. What impact did I have on their lives? In what ways did I influence those young people? Were they influenced not only by the skills that I taught them and the knowledge that I imparted to them, but also by the quality of my life? In most cases, I do not know. I suspect that I am not meant to know, but I hope that they were inspired in ways that went beyond the subject matter that I taught. And, of course, it was not just those young people that I encountered – I met most of their parents, most of them many times, and then there were my teaching colleagues with whom I was in daily contact. What influence did I have on those lives? Did they see, displayed in me, the kind of change that I would like to see in this world?

Of course, the influence that we have on the world, our legacy if you want to use that word, is not restricted to our career. Indeed, it touches everyone that we meet – our friends, our family, our neighbours, even just people we pass in the street or stand next to at the supermarket checkout. It manifests itself in the smiles and the courtesies that we have for those we meet, the helping hand for neighbours, the kindness we show to strangers. All of this adds up to that personal impact that we have on the world and on the people we meet.

For many people, most people, the influence that they will have upon the world touches, first and foremost, their children. Although, as I have said earlier, I have no children myself, I recognise that parents are faced with both an enormous privilege and an enormous responsibility to ensure that they pass on the very best moral and ethical legacy to their children. One of the most important responsibilities of parents, I believe, is to be the best and most positive role model that they can be for their children. As children mature and become young adults, many are seduced by a more secular *laissez-faire* lifestyle, often to the disappointment of their parents. The influences of peer-groups and of the secular world are strong and tantalising, and the task of counter-balancing those secular influences falls primarily, although not exclusively, upon parents. Yes, you may be disappointed if your children gravitate away from your influence and towards a more secular lifestyle, but where the proper groundwork has been done, where a loving role model has been displayed, where ethical and spiritual values have been taught, many of those young people will later return to take up the legacy of their parents, and to create their own spiritual legacies.

Parents, teach your children well! Be an affirmative and supportive source of guidance in their lives. Teach them and guide them constantly in the paths of righteousness because every day they will be faced with persuasive peer group pressures to conform to the standards and normal practices of the secular world. In the Old Testament, before the Israelites crossed the Jordan and entered the promised land, which Moses himself would not enter, Moses wanted to impress upon the Israelites the importance of teaching their children to love God:

> *These commandments that I give you today are to be on your hearts. Impress them on your children. Talk about them when you sit at home and when you walk along the road, when you lie down and when you get up. Tie them as symbols on your hands and bind them on your foreheads. Write them on the doorframes of your houses and on your gates.*[2]

The role and responsibility of parents in passing the truths of righteousness to their children and to their grandchildren was being emphasised by Moses and is also recognised in the New Testament Scriptures. Timothy was a young man who Paul had taken under his wing as his protégé, and in a letter to Timothy, Paul wrote:

> *I am reminded of your sincere faith, which first lived in your grandmother Lois and in your mother Eunice and, I am persuaded, now lives in you also.*[3]

Timothy had been given a legacy of faith from his mother and from his grandmother, and Paul recognised the positive influence that legacy had on the young Timothy. There can be no doubt that God wants us to pass on a spiritual legacy to future generations, and the lives of our children and of their children will function better and be more righteous for having been given such a legacy.

I challenge you to think about your life, about the impact that you have had, and are having, and will have, on those around you. Do you know that your life matters? Are you choosing to live a life which will leave the world a better place because you have passed through it?

* Have you spread hope and optimism in this world?
* Have you always made people feel valued and cared for?
* Have you displayed patience when others are testing that patience?
* Have you been tolerant of others even when you disagreed with them?

- Have you always lifted people up and always chosen not to put people down – have you chosen not to do things or to say things that diminish the personal self-respect of others?
- Have you always chosen to forgive people, to tell them that you forgive them, and to move on?
- Have you helped transform the lives of others in a way that has made their life richer and more joyful?
- Have you intervened to bring peace to personal conflicts between others?
- Have you added to the wellspring of joy and happiness in this world?
- Have you opened doors and made it possible for others to follow their dreams?
- Have you inspired others to be the best person that they can be?
- Have you shared your blessings with others? Have you shared your wealth, your skills, your time, even just a smile of acknowledgement to a stranger?
- Have you encouraged others to do likewise, so that they, too, can leave this world a better place?

Perhaps you can answer 'yes' to all those questions and, if so, I commend you and I applaud you. If you are like most people, however, me included, then you probably have a few of those questions to work on. And that is fine. God is giving us time to work on those things, he is giving us time to make a difference in this world.

Sadly, from my perspective, many people do not turn their minds to such considerations until the latter years of their lives. In our youth, many of us find that life provides such an egocentric offering that we are too distracted to focus on the question of how our lives may be impacting on others. And I, myself, must plead guilty to this – to having lived too many years with an egocentric attitude towards life, and to having wasted some of my limited time on this earth. I know, from personal experience, that there are few things sadder than looking back on wasted years, and so I encourage younger readers to consider, now, the legacy that they are leaving. I urge you, do not leave it until it is too late to make a meaningful change.

Speaking on this issue, the late Dr. Billy Graham, perhaps the best-known evangelist of the 20th century, has said:

> Our days are numbered. One of the primary goals in our lives should be to prepare for our last day. The legacy we leave is not just in our possessions, but in the quality of our lives. What preparations should we be making now? The greatest waste in all of our earth, which cannot be recycled or reclaimed, is our waste of the time that God has given us each day.[4]

Every one of us will leave a legacy; yours may be a positive legacy for good that puts your children on the pathway to fulfillment and happiness, or it may be a legacy that negatively influences your children and others. Furthermore, the legacy that you leave may be, in fact frequently is, self-perpetuating. If you leave a negative influence on your children it is likely that they will, in turn, leave a negative influence on your grandchildren. If you impart values and truths to your children, if you pass on a positive legacy to your children, then that is likely to endure through future generations. So, set the direction of your legacy now. You have a wonderful and valuable story to tell. You have a positive and life-enriching legacy to leave. Now is the time to be working on that legacy.

1. *The Complete Writings of Mahatma Gandhi, Vol. 13*, Ch. 153, page 241, published in 1913
2. Deuteronomy 6:6-9
3. 2 Timothy 1:5
4. *The Enduring Classics of Billy Graham* (ed. Thomas Nelson Inc, 2004) - ISBN: 9781418515027

Chapter 11
Live a Life of Hope

Blessed are you when people hate you, when they exclude you and insult you and reject your name as evil, because of the Son of Man. Rejoice in that day and leap for joy, because great is your reward in heaven[1]

For it has been granted to you that for the sake of Christ you should not only believe in him but also suffer for his sake[2]

Consider it pure joy, my brothers and sisters, whenever you face trials of many kinds[3]

Do not be surprised at the fiery ordeal that has come on you to test you, as though something strange were happening to you. But rejoice inasmuch as you participate in the sufferings of Christ[4]

Now I rejoice in my sufferings for your sake[5]

Jesus tells us to 'leap for joy' when we face troubles and suffering[6], and throughout the New Testament the apostles are telling us to rejoice in our suffering. Yeah, right!

For many people, the concept of rejoicing in suffering is nothing less than counterintuitive nonsense. And I do not blame them for feeling that way. Suffering, be it physical suffering or psychological suffering is something that besets all of us from time to time, but most sane people would like it to be something which is encountered as infrequently as possible. Thus, the concept of rejoicing in suffering seems so illogical and unreasonable, preposterous even, that we are left wondering just why we are instructed to do so. What are the New Testament writers getting at here? Are we just being told to be stoic in the face of troubles, to keep a stiff upper-lip and just hang in there? Is it something beyond that, perhaps even masochism that is expected of us, or is it something else, something that we are missing here?

Some people believe that, in times of trouble and suffering, if they just tough it out and keep smiling then they are obeying this instruction to rejoice in their suffering. Indeed, some seem to welcome such suffering, or desire an increase in their afflictions, so that they might better display their stoicism. Such people are misguided and are misinterpreting these scriptures. I doubt that the apostle Paul, during times of imprisonment, floggings and persecution was leaping for joy and praying 'Bring it on, Lord! I can take more than this.' Stoicism is an admirable trait, but it is not what is meant when the Scriptures speak of 'rejoicing in suffering'.

It is instructive to remember that many of the New Testament writers, and particularly Peter, were writing to the church when it was undergoing times of extreme persecution. The mad Emperor Nero was persecuting Christians to the point of death; having them killed in the Colosseum for public entertainment and turning them into human torches to light the streets of Rome. And to those Christians, as we have seen, Peter wrote:

> *Do not be surprised at the fiery ordeal that has come on you to test you, as though something strange were happening to you. But rejoice inasmuch as you participate in the sufferings of Christ.*[7]

It is impossible for us to put ourselves into the mindset of those Christians to whom Peter was writing, but I find Peter's words *'as though something strange were happening to you'* to be somewhat confronting. It almost seems that Peter was saying to them, 'There is nothing strange or unusual about this persecution. For followers of Christ, this is the new-normal.' Now, it is most unlikely that we will ever have to face persecution on such a level, and we should thank God for that, daily, but I think that when Peter wrote *'but rejoice inasmuch as you participate in the sufferings of Christ'* that he meant something far beyond an appeal for stoic acceptance of this new realty. The question of just what was meant by Peter and the other apostles who called for rejoicing in suffering is something that we will return to shortly.

But before we turn our minds to what the apostles were saying, we should look at another category of misguided belief in respect to the call to rejoice in suffering. Some people take it further than stoicism and believe that to 'rejoice in suffering' they are expected to enjoy pain, be it physical pain or psychological pain. Indeed, some even engage in self-flagellation, whipping themselves to inflict physical pain in the misguided belief that they are pleasing God by the level of their rejoicing in such suffering. Such people are masochists, and their confidence in the worth of physical self-flagellation as a way of expressing their spirituality could not be further from the truth.

There are also people whom I would refer to as psychological masochists – those who rejoice in the terrible and tragic circumstances to which we are all subjected from time to time. Suffering, whether it be physical or psychological suffering, as we have seen, is something that we all must endure in this fallen world. Sadly, if not responded to in the correct way, such suffering can even make one question the very existence of God and of his purpose for our lives.

In an earlier chapter I related the tragic story of my sister's death and I mentioned there that I still have occasions when I am reminded of those tragic circumstances, and that on those occasions I sometimes feel some guilt – a feeling that I should have been a better brother and that I should have been able to do more to prevent my sister's death. Such thoughts and such feelings, I believe, are a natural response when our hearts are hurting, and mine is still hurting. But fortunately for me those occurrences are becoming less and less frequent and less and less intense with the passing of time. There is, however, a line to be drawn between the natural occurrence of painful memories like that, and the actions of the psychological masochist who takes tragic circumstances and heartache to a different level and uses them for a different purpose.

The psychological masochist welcomes such heartache, perpetuates it and wallows in it, sometimes believing that doing so is a projection of his or her obedience to the New Testament call for rejoicing in suffering.

We have all known people like that. Perhaps you have not known people who take physical masochism to the point of self-flagellation, but I am sure that most readers would have known those who wallow in their physical and psychological pain almost as if they take pride in torturing their bodies and their minds. To do so, in the belief that one is being obedient to the scriptural call to 'rejoice in suffering' is a distorted and perverted interpretation of Scripture. It is the belief that righteousness comes through one's own pain and shame. Our God is a God of love, and he just doesn't want that from us. But too many people settle for less than God's plan for their lives. They have become used to their pain and suffering, and they dwell in it, they enjoy it. There are close parallels here between people who live like this, and the non-thinking pessimists spoken of in the first chapter of this book. Both seem to welcome, even to seek out, bad news and difficult times, and to delight in it. To rejoice in our suffering does not mean to enjoy it or to be glad that it has occurred. Suffering is never fun – don't try and make it so.

Pain, troubles, and suffering in this fallen world are unavoidable. Remember the words of Jesus, *'In this world you will have trouble'*.[8] We will all know deep heartache, we will all know both physical and psychological pain, and all of us will experience the death of our current physical bodies, some in the most terrible and agonising circumstances. One simple question is being asked here; how are you going to respond to that suffering? By rejoicing in it? Yes, by rejoicing in it! But how? If rejoicing in suffering is not simple stoicism, and if it is not masochism, then what is it? What are we expected to do? The apostle Paul spells it out thus:

We rejoice in our sufferings, knowing that suffering produces endurance, and endurance produces character, and character

> *produces hope, and hope does not put us to shame, because God's love has been poured into our hearts through the Holy Spirit who has been given to us.*[9]

To me, the most important word in those verses of Scripture is the word 'hope'. We do not rejoice because we are going though troublesome and painful times; we rejoice not because of those things, but in spite of them. We rejoice because we know that we have hope – hope that will not fail us ('not put us to shame', in Paul's words), hope that we have because of the love of God, which has been shown to us by the Lord Jesus Christ, and which has been poured into our hearts by the Holy Spirit.

A word of interpretation here: when Paul uses the word 'hope' he is not speaking of some desired outcome which might or might not happen – something about which there is no certainty. In today's culture you may hear someone say, 'I sure hope that I win the lottery'. That is an expression of hope, with uncertainty. There is nothing certain about that. You should not think that is the word that Paul was using in these Scriptures. Paul uses the word 'hope' as a synonym of faith and confidence. We are not sure who wrote the book in the Bible which is known as the letter to the Hebrews. It may well also have been Paul, but whoever it was that writer wrote:

> *Faith is confidence in what we hope for and assurance about what we do not see.*[10]

Do you see the pattern being formulated here?

Faith…....confidence……hope……assurance

There is that word 'hope' again. For Paul, and for Christians today, our hope is grounded and anchored in our faith in God, it is the confidence that comes from knowing the nature of God and it is the assurance of God's faithfulness which is poured out to us by the Holy Spirit. It is thus an expression of absolute certainty.

Without that hope, suffering would be just an end in itself. It would be ongoing and meaningless suffering. In this fallen world we cannot avoid suffering but we should face that suffering with faith and with hope. Suffering without faith and without hope is devastating, it will break your spirit. It can even convince you that there is no God, or at least not a God that loves and cares for you. It can turn you away from God – I know, I have been there, as I have related earlier. But, as we have seen in Paul's letter to the church in Rome,[11] suffering in faith gives us the power to endure, and endurance, says Paul creates our character. Our character shows who we are – it shows, if we are faithful, that we are a child of God, and that we are his eternally – and that is from whence we get our hope.

I related, in Chapter 2, that in my suffering I had reached the point of screaming at God and telling him that he does not exist. I am not sure that, at that point, I really believed that God didn't exist, but I certainly felt that he didn't love me – I was feeling estranged from God. I have little doubt that many of my readers will be able to relate to that feeling of being at arms-length from God.

I think the disciple Peter experienced something similar to this feeling of being estranged from God after the crucifixion of Jesus. Peter had sworn that he would never abandon Jesus. Prior to the arrest of Jesus, Peter had declared *'Even if all fall away on account of you, I never will'*.[12] Jesus' response to Peter was to say *'I tell you, Peter, before the rooster crows today, you will deny three times that you know me'*[13] and Peter had then gone on to declare *'even if I have to die with you, I will never disown you.'*[14]

A few short hours later Peter was standing around a fire in the courtyard of Caiaphas, the High Priest whilst Jesus was being tried before the Sanhedrin. Three times, around that fire, Peter was asked whether he was one of Jesus' followers, and three times he denied that he knew Jesus. Immediately after his third denial the rooster crowed, and Jesus turned to look straight at Peter.[15] I have no doubt that when Jesus turned and looked at Peter, he looked with love and with compassion, but I doubt that Peter interpreted it that way. That glance from Jesus must have been devastating for Peter, and we are told that he went outside and wept bitterly.[16] 'I couldn't keep my promise to him, I couldn't stand by him, I've failed him, I've denied I even knew him, **and he knows!**'

In so many ways I see myself in Peter. I do not mean in the outspoken and unrestrained Peter, for I am certainly an introvert. Peter could never be called an introvert. But I see myself making the same mistakes that Peter made, saying the wrong thing at the wrong time, and making promises that I cannot keep. At times, Peter seemed to be on something of a roller-coaster ride in his relationship with Jesus – sometimes it was such a close relationship, but at other times Peter must have felt that a huge gulf had opened up between himself and the Lord. I know that feeling, I can relate to that too.

On the third day after the crucifixion, on the first day of the week, Mary Magdalene went to the tomb and saw that the stone had been removed from the entrance. When she looked inside the tomb and saw that it was empty, she then ran to tell this news to Peter and John.[17] Peter and John then started out for the tomb, both running, but John outran Peter and reached the tomb first. John looked inside the tomb, but did not go in. Then Peter arrived and went straight into the tomb where he saw that the tomb was indeed empty, apart from the cloths in which the body of Jesus had been wrapped.[18] The Bible tells us that *'Finally the other disciple, who had reached the tomb first* (John), *also went inside. He saw and believed'.*[19] John saw, and he believed! We are not told what Peter was thinking but I am sure that his mind was in turmoil. What was going through his troubled and despondent mind as he stood there in that empty tomb? What had Peter been thinking as he ran to the tomb? We cannot know, but it may even be that it was those thoughts that accounted for why Peter ran slower than John. Perhaps his heart was not really in it; 'Even if he is alive, it won't be the same! I denied him, and **he knows!**'

During the next week, the risen Jesus appeared twice to the disciples, both times in the locked room where they were staying. On the first occasion, Thomas was not with them, but Peter was present on both occasions. We are told that *'the disciples were overjoyed when they saw the Lord.'*[20] We are not told what the disciples said on these occasions, nor are we told what Peter was thinking, but I am sure that Peter's mind was troubled. Surely, Peter had something to say! Peter *always* had something to say! Boisterous, outspoken, rambunctious Peter, the one who opens his mouth to change feet – surely, he had *something* to say! Perhaps he did, but it is not recorded. It is possible, and not unreasonable to imagine, that Peter may have been standing back a little, something totally out of character for Peter, and perhaps his mind was spinning with bitter memories. ......**he knows!**

All those incidents where I have spoken of what Peter may have been feeling and thinking are, of course, speculation. We cannot be sure what he was thinking, but we do know that Jesus found it necessary to reinstate Peter, to restore his relationship with Peter, and to renew his faith. It happened by the shore of the sea of Galilee. Peter and some of the other disciples had taken their boat out on Galilee to catch fish, but they had caught nothing. The risen Jesus appeared standing on the shore and called out telling them to cast their net on the other side of the boat. At that point, they did not recognise that it was Jesus, but when they did cast their net on the other side it was filled with so many fish that *'they were unable to haul the net in.'*[21] It was at that point that John declared *'It is the Lord!'* Though they were about 100 yards from shore, Peter jumped overboard and rushed ashore.

Breakfast was prepared on the shore – fish and bread cooked on a fire which Jesus had prepared. But not just any fire! Throughout Scripture, the word for 'fire' is used many times, but there are only two verses in all of Scripture which use the word *anthrakia (ἀνθρακιὰν)* – specifically, 'a charcoal fire'.[22] Charcoal has a distinct aroma, and I am sure that the aroma of that fire, carried by the sea breeze, triggered in Peter's mind the memory of when he had last stood around a charcoal fire. That last occasion, the only other place in all Scripture where a 'charcoal fire' is specifically mentioned, was when Peter had stood around a charcoal fire in Caiaphas' courtyard, where he had three times denied that he knew Jesus. Oh, the bitter memories of his denials - **He knows!**

After breakfast, Jesus draws Peter aside and the conversation which follows is crucial for the reinstatement of Peter, and for the rest of his life.

I am a translator by vocation, and I know that sometimes things are lost in translation. English is, at times, a limited and inadequate language and something critical is lost in the English translation of this conversation. Greek, the language of the New Testament, knows four different words meaning 'love'. There is **philia** (φιλία), best translated as brotherly love or friendship; there is **storge** (στοργή) translated as a familial love of natural affection; there is **eros** (ερως), a passionate and romantic love as between a man and his wife, and there is **agapé** (ἀγάπη), the highest form or love, the love originating from God for man and the reciprocal love of man for God. We must bear those differences in mind when we read this conversation between Jesus and Peter.

> *'Simon son of John, do you love me more than these?'*
> *'Yes, Lord', he said, 'you know that I love you.'*
> *Jesus said, 'Feed my lambs.'* [23]

In English, that seems straight forward, but when Jesus asked Peter here, 'do you love me?' he used the Greek verb 'agapas'. 'Do you love me with that agapé love, with that total and sacrificial form of love?' But Peter could not commit to that. When Peter replied he used the verb 'philiō'. 'Yes, Lord, you know that I love you as a brother.' Jesus did not say 'Well, that's not good enough, Peter. I demand more than that'. Instead, Jesus gave Peter a task, a commission, 'Feed my lambs'. We will return to the significance of that commission shortly.

A second time Jesus asked Peter:
'Simon son of John, do you love me?'
Agapas again; Do you love me with agapé love?
He answered, 'Yes, Lord, you know that I love you'.
Philio again; Yes, Lord, you know that I love you as a brother.
Jesus said, 'Take care of my sheep.' [24]

A third time Jesus asked this question. Three denials – three questions.
'Simon son of John, do you love me?'
But this time Jesus came down to Peter's level and used the verb 'philio'. Do you love me as a brother?
He said, 'Lord, you know all things; you know that I love you'.
Yes, Lord, you know that I love you as a brother.
Jesus said, 'Feed my sheep.' [25]

By coming down to Peter's level, Jesus was, in effect, saying to Peter, 'Okay Peter, if that is where you are at, we'll take it from there. So, get back on your feet, for I have a job for you – Feed my lambs. Take care of my sheep. Feed my sheep'. When you've let someone down there is nothing that can better assure you that you have been forgiven, than for that person to give you an important job to do, and to trust you to do it. Peter has been restored and has been entrusted with a vital job for the rest of his life – to take care of and to nurture the church. It is a role that he would fulfill with distinction.

Earlier, in the region of Caesarea Philippi, Jesus had asked the disciples *'Who do you say that I am?'* and Peter had answered *'You are the Christ, the Son of the Living God.'* [26] Jesus then said to Peter:

> *Blessed are you, Simon son of Jonah, for this was not revealed to you by flesh and blood, but by my Father in heaven. And I tell you that you are Peter, and on this rock I will build my church, and the gates of Hades will not overcome it.* ²⁷

When Peter first met Jesus, Peter's name had been Simon, but Jesus had decided to call him Peter, which originates from the Aramaic 'Cephas' and from the Greek 'Πετρος' (Petros), both meaning 'rock'. Jesus had given him this name because Peter was to be the rock upon which the Christian church would be built. '*And the gates of Hades* (hell) *will not overcome it,*' Jesus said. And neither would Peter's denials mean that the promise would be revoked. That promise, as with all promises of God, was set in stone (no pun intended), and by the shore of Galilee Peter was reinstated and commissioned to get on with the work. In that conversation following breakfast on the shore of Galilee, Jesus was in effect saying to Peter, 'Get back up on your feet again, Peter. Hope again, live again, work again'.

Peter would go on to be one of the apostles who would call upon Christians to rejoice in their suffering, because he knew that through suffering one could find hope. He had been there and done that! Peter had wallowed in his troubles, he had felt unloved, probably felt rejected, broken, and worthless, but he had found the absolute assurance of hope that Christ gives. It is the hope that comes from believing that you have worth, great worth, because you are God's unique creation and because you are greatly loved. And it is hope based in the knowledge that God does not pull us down – he builds us up!

I said earlier that I can see much of myself in Peter. I, too, have made promises to the Lord that I have been unable to keep. I, too, have stumbled and bumbled through my relationship with him, making the same stupid mistakes repeatedly. I too have not loved him as I should. I have failed my Lord, and far more than three times. And yet, Jesus has not said to me 'Okay, Ian. That's it!

You have blown it too many times.' Rather, he has said to me 'Okay, Ian. If that is where you are at, I am there with you. Get up on your feet, hope again, and we'll go forward together'. Such is grace and the love of God. Such is hope.

My entire intent and purpose in this book has been to bring a message of hope for every reader, Christian and non-Christian alike. But I are not naïve, and I know that for those who do not know Jesus Christ the idea of rejoicing in suffering is nonsense, because they have no hope – they do not have the hope that only Jesus can bring to their life. As we reach the end of this chapter, and the end of this book, I pray that, if you are not already a follower of Jesus Christ, that you will turn to him, put your faith in him, and be blessed with that hope. Yes, you will still face heartache and challenging circumstances, but your response need not be one of despair. In closing, I can think of no better words than those of Charles Swindoll:

> *If we will only believe and ask, a full measure of God's grace and peace is available to any of us. By the wonderful, prevailing mercy of God, we can find purpose in the scattering and sadness of our lives. We can not only deal with suffering but rejoice through it.* [28]

It is my prayer and my hope that you, too, will know God's grace, and the hope that Jesus gives.

1. Luke 6:22-23
2. Philippians 1:29
3. James 1:2
4. 1 Peter 4:12-13
5. Colossians 1:24
6. Luke 6:22-23
7. 1 Peter *op-cit*
8. John 16:23
9. Romans 5:3-5 ESV
10. Hebrews 11:1
11. Romans *op-cit*
12. Matthew 26:33
13. Luke 22:34
14. Matthew 26:35
15. Luke 22:61
16. Luke 22:62
17. John 20:1-2
18. John 20:3-6
19. John 20:8
20. John 20:20
21. John 21:6
22. John 18:19 & 21:9 (NLT, ESV, AMSV, AB)
23. John 21:15
24. John 21:16
25. John 21:7
26. Mathew 16:15-16
27. Matthew 16:17-18
28. Swindoll, C. *Hope Again (Ch2.)*

BIBLIOGRAPHY

Morton, Brian
Falser Words Were Never Spoken
New York Times, 30 August 2011

Stroom, G. van der & Massotty, S. (Eds.)
Anne Frank's Tales from The Secret Annex,
Halban, London, 2010

Shapiro, Fred R. (Ed.)
Yale Book of Quotations
Yale University Press, New Haven, 2006

Swindoll, Charles R.
Laugh Again - Hope Again; Two Books to Inspire a Joy-Filled Life
Thomas Nelson, Nashville, 1996

Theopedia
An Encyclopedia of Biblical Christianity
https://www.theopedia.com/

www.ingramcontent.com/pod-product-compliance
Lightning Source LLC
LaVergne TN
LVHW011710060526
838200LV00051B/2846